OVERWEIGHT TEENAGERS

Don't Bear the Burden Alone

MICHAEL D. LeBOW, Ph.D.

Foreword by
J. Kevin Thompson, Ph.D.

INSIGHT BOOKS
PLENUM PRESS • NEW YORK AND LONDON

Library of Congress Cataloging-in-Publication Data

On file

ISBN 0-306-45047-X

© 1995 Plenum Press, New York
Insight Books is a Division of Plenum Publishing Corporation
233 Spring Street, New York, N.Y. 10013-1578

An Insight Book

10 9 8 7 6 5 4 3 2 1

Printed in the United States of America

TO ESTY AND JULIE
MY SISTERS, MY FRIENDS

FOREWORD ───────────────

If you've ever felt the pain of being overweight, of being teased by friends, of being left out of games and social activities, then read this book. This book is written for you—the teenager. That is why it is such a special book. Actually, that is just one of many reasons. This book is special because it is written by Dr. Michael LeBow, one of the foremost researchers in the treatment of childhood, adolescent, and teenage weight problems. However, just because he is an expert doesn't mean that this book is filled with difficult-to-follow technical details. Quite the contrary. Dr. LeBow's program and guidelines are provided along with clearcut examples based on your concerns, hopes, fears, and daily struggles.

After just a few pages, you'll realize another important reason to read this book. Dr. LeBow has "been there." He tells of coping "when I was about 12 years old, fat, and the butt of fat jokes." He remembers a friend who told him, "You'd really be nice looking, if you'd lose 40 pounds." Dr. LeBow knows that much of the pain from being overweight comes from interpersonal rejection. His focus on this area is just one of the reasons I was honored to be asked to write this introduction. For many years, my own research has focused on the damaging effects of teasing on one's body image and self-esteem.

Before going on to discuss how this book may change your life and the entire way you approach weight control, let's pause for a moment. Perhaps you aren't a teenager. Maybe you picked up this book because you're a parent who is worried about a son or daughter. Or perhaps you are a therapist—a physician, psychologist, social worker, dietician, or any of a variety of other types of clinicians who work with teenagers with weight problems. If so, you've found an invaluable resource.

If you doubt my word, skip ahead to Chapter 10 and scan Dr. LeBow's discussion of your role in the management of your teenager's (or patient's) weight problem. If you still doubt my word, begin to read this book. You'll quickly realize that Dr. LeBow's presentation dramatically helps you understand the distress of the overweight teenager. You'll also find the background and techniques easy to follow yet based on firm scientific evidence. If you're a parent, buy this book for your teenager. If you're a therapist, buy it for your patients (or, buy it and use the techniques in your own treatment programs).

Now, where was I? Oh, yes. As I mentioned earlier, Dr. LeBow has written this book for you—the teenager. We know this because he uses the title "Teens in Charge" for several chapters. Before considering the treatments illustrated in the later chapters, however, let's look quickly at the material covered in the first three chapters. In Chapter 1, two teenagers, Michael and Margaret, describe in their own words the experience of being overweight. This is followed in Chapter 2 by a presentation of how the body stores calories and fat and of ways to increase energy expenditure to lose weight. Chapter 3 examines the many dangers of extreme methods of weight loss (such as fasting and fad dieting) as well as the usual outcomes of these techniques—eating disorders.

Chapter 4 focuses on preparation for beginning the program by helping you answer a variety of questions, including: Am I heavy? Am I fat? Will my problems disappear if I trim down? Do I want to trim down? Chapter 5 presents the how-to of record-keeping for eating and exercise activities. Importantly, some easy-to-follow and scientifically proven diet plans, such as the traffic light diet developed by Leonard Epstein and colleagues, are explained.

A shift in tone is taken in Chapter 6, which begins a focus on the psychological aspects of weight control. However, the approach used is not one of traditional psychotherapy, which might focus on a supposed deep-rooted neurosis or conflict. (In fact, research shows that there are minimal psychological differences between overweight and normal-weight individuals.) Instead, and appropriately, Dr. LeBow discusses the role of "positives" in the control of eating behavior. This use of reinforcement principles is the hallmark of a successful weight-loss program.

Chapter 7 also focuses on psychological issues, beginning with methods to control "nasty self-talk." The importance of thinking constructively is essential to modifying old patterns related to overeating. For example, you may have thought, "I'm fat and ugly and I'll always be fat and ugly." If you restructure this to, "I'm overweight, but I'm not ugly," you can immediately see how self-esteem might benefit. Chapter 7 also includes effective ways of rearranging your home and school environment to enhance control of eating.

I'm not sure it's necessary to detail any more of the components of Dr. LeBow's program. I'll leave you to discover, on your own, the procedures for making a contract with yourself, planning meals and exercise, removing stumbling blocks, and coping with relapse. I should note, however, that you get more than just trite phrases and encouragements from this book. You get specific details and guidelines. You get tables and graphs and figures and diet plans and activity sheets . . . you get the idea.

But most importantly, as I mentioned at the beginning of this foreword to *Overweight Teenagers,* you get a teenager's perspective. Dr. LeBow does not talk down to you. He doesn't stand over you with a set of instructions and an attitude. What he *does* do is understand your situation. He's been there, and he knows about the pain—and the scars. He's devoted his life's work to helping you with your pain and scars. In this book, he's brought together the essential strategies to help you begin the healing process. The rest is up to you. Take his advice and become a "teen in charge" of your life.

J. Kevin Thompson, Ph.D.

University of South Florida
Tampa, Florida

ACKNOWLEDGMENTS ——————

I'm indebted to the scientists and practitioners whose work I've cited throughout. I'm also indebted to the teenagers I've treated over the years, composite examples included herein.

At this time, I wish to thank my editor at Insight Books, Frank Darmstadt, for repeatedly alerting me to writings on teenage overweight. His diligence has helped me immensely.

I thank Bill and Matt LeBow for sharing with me their views on weight, diet, and exercise. Special credit goes to Matt for reading this book from the teenage perspective and for making improvements.

I thank Mildred Boudreau, who many years ago taught me to recognize and battle the teenage antifat environment. And I thank Barbara LeBow, who today teaches me how to fight in a different war, one I must win in order to free myself to do the work I do.

CONTENTS ———————

CHAPTER 4

TEENS IN CHARGE: PREPARING YOURSELF 61

CHAPTER 5

TEENS IN CHARGE: WATCH YOURSELF AND MAKE RECORDS 85

CHAPTER 6

TEENS IN CHARGE: USING POSITIVES............... 107

CHAPTER 7

TEENS IN CHARGE: THINKING, REARRANGING, CONTRACTING, AND ASSERTING TO CONTROL OVERWEIGHT.. 125

CHAPTER 9

PROBLEMS GETTING AND STAYING WHERE YOU WANT

CHAPTER 10

FOR PARENTS AND PROFESSIONALS

CONTENTS —————————————— XIX

CHAPTER 1

MEET MICHAEL AND MARGARET

Is this book about a rare physical condition? No. Definitely no. If you are between the ages of 12 and 17 and are obese (and I use that word not to be crude, insensitive, or mean), you have company. Recent estimates are that about 3.5 million fat teenagers live in the United States. And of them about 1.3 million are fat enough to be regarded as super-obese, according to Dr. William Dietz of Tufts University Medical School.[1]

Should they begin a program of watching what they eat and becoming more active? Should they take specific, planned steps to slim down? Some scientists and thera-pists answer yes to both questions, others are uncertain, and still others say no. After reading this book and conferring with your physician, you decide what is best for you.

MICHAEL

It was in the third week of June that Michael entered our buzzing, thin-crazy world. Normal and healthy, he was 8 pounds, 21 inches. Six months later, having undergone six months of overfeeding, he was 30 pounds. His well-meaning and loving feeders, mother and father, praised his fast growth. They adored him, as did their friends, neighbors, and relatives. His round full face framed in curly black hair and his soft and cuddly body made him irresistible. Wherever he was—grandmother's, grocery store, mall, park—he captured the "ooh's" and "aah's" that follow beautiful babies. Everyone beyond the age of four succumbed to his charisma; cute was his middle name.

In Michael's family, chubbiness was healthiness. And making Michael chubby and healthy was a joy. In his third month, when he began solids, Michael learned the first of several soon-to-be-mastered eating games: Dad would sit directly in front of Michael, who, secured in his high chair, would be noisily waiting. The food tray, which held apple sauce, pureed carrots, and pureed chicken, or an equally nutritious display, would be on the kitchen table to Dad's immediate right. Filled spoon in hand, Dad would lift the utensil high and, angling it downward toward Michael's open mouth, would say (against the background noise of the loud droning airplane-sounds Dad made), "Are you ready, here it comes, eat it all." Michael would. Immediately, Dad would praise him, "Oh, Michael's such a good boy!" No finicky eater, son delighted father—emptied dishes, refused food rarely. The game, "Make eating fun," worked too well. Michael learned that his eating and goodness had something to do with each other, though what, never would he discover. And he learned that his eating pleased others, though why, never would he know.

There would be other eating games, such as "Eat if you want friendship," "Eat if you want to celebrate," and "Eat if you've denied yourself," but the rules that governed them, chances to play them, and fallout from them would come later.

By his fifth year, Michael still captivated relatives and neighbors with his angelic face and chubby body. But this was the year trouble came. It was the start of a 13-year sentence handed down for a crime he neither committed nor understood. His punishment: incessant and interminable, peer-sponsored antifat attacks. His first incarceration, kindergarten, trapped him in a world of young fatness-defilers. Dressed in shorts and knit polo shirts, his bulging flesh accented, Michael unwittingly invited the youthful offenders to offend. He became "Fatty" to peers, who punched, pushed, ridiculed, and rejected him. They hated his shape and told him so. He felt miserable.

He would find the rest of grade school to be even worse:

> My first grade teacher opened up my eyes, making me realize that what my parents called my healthiness and my robustness might be something more. She engineered my being elected that year's Santa Claus. Her reasoning was simple. As she put it to the class, "He (meaning me) has more meat on his bones!" I liked the idea of being Santa Claus because everyone else wanted to be it. The joys were passing out gifts, wearing a special costume, and receiving lots of attention. But there were drawbacks, too. Indeed, something felt wrong with the whole thing.
>
> I felt uneasy. I sensed that my parents were not overjoyed either when I explained why I was chosen, namely that the meat on my bones won me the honor.
>
> In time my position in grade school, and for that matter everywhere else, became sharper. I was the fat

one, or more accurately one of the "fatties." I didn't really like the other blimps because they looked funny, especially when they played football and base-ball. And, most of all, nobody who was anybody liked them.

My friends called me names, too. I inured to their epithets, however, and at least until the fourth grade took my greater size to mean greater strength. But in the sixth grade I learned something new: fatness was not toughness. All of the thin kids who fought me, beat me!

The kings were the guys with the V shapes. Stan, to name one, had noticeable muscular contours. Four of these "royals" allowed me to enter their kingdom, primarily as court jester. I thought that if I could get them to laugh, I could get them to accept. I was wrong.

They teased and they tricked. Once they told me to go home for my swim trunks, and we would all go to La Cienaga pool; yet when I returned to the meeting place, everyone had left. I forgave them for ditching me, because at that time in my life it was simpler to forgive such abuse.

My first job was delivering papers. It was boring, but at least you could hide your front and back sides with the paper sack. Selling papers on the street corner was more lucrative, yet more visible, and hence more painful. You couldn't snack there because people looked at you as if to say fat boys should never eat.

Once I was a busboy at a fancy department store restaurant. The worst thing about the job was the white uniform. For some reason, the establishment thought boys should have tubelike waists and snake-like hips. The uniform chafed, and I looked strange waddling around in it. I quit the job within two weeks.[2]

For Michael, junior high proved no safer than grade school. Fatness-defilers, like graffiti on tunnel walls, surrounded him, engulfed him, choked him—in the classroom, in the nurse's office, in the teachers' lounge, in the hall. Still fat with great visibility in a community still antifat with great enthusiasm, Michael, now 5 feet 2 inches, 170 pounds, salved his hurts with endless television and bounteous snacks.

I liked sports in junior high, but never could make the first team. The coach, who was also my math teacher, was a V-shape who wore his shirt two buttons open at the top, when the weather permitted. He didn't like fat kids, of that I was certain. Being a no-nonsense guy about football, basketball, and baseball, his formula was simple: if you were not good enough, you were no good.

I felt bad about being second-rate in his eyes and just accepted his denigration. He represented the zenith, the model man, who continually tried to prove that fatness was weakness. And he represented the leader of the best I so longed to be one of. Organized sports eventually became punishing, so I stopped trying out for the teams. Even after-school sports became shaming, for often I was the one who went on the side that had exhausted its choices but needed one more player.[3]

As junior high faded into a bad memory, Michael moved into tenth grade. High school, the remaining three years of his prison sentence, made the three previous years seem lenient.

High school was my nightmare. One day during swimming the coach yelled, "Everybody out of the pool," and like regimented troops, all the V-shapes pulled up with great ease. I couldn't get out. The laughter was deafening. I laughed as loudly as everyone else did. Is there a choice?

For some strange reason I had a mandatory wrestling class in tenth grade. More of an inverted V-shape like me but strong and sturdy unlike me, the teacher adored his mightiness and with equal intensity hated my fatness, which he saw as weakness. So, he demonstrated holds on me. I weighed over 200 pounds then and was halfway between five and six feet—the perfect patsy for him. Appreciating my dilemma, my doctor wrote me an excuse from gym; aperiodic asthma saved me. I never returned to gym and in so doing cut off one source of the fitness I desperately needed.[4]

It was at this time I first saw Jean Ray, the girl of my fantasy. She was irresistible—5 feet 3 inches tall, long brown hair, large brown eyes, full lips, porcelain-like skin, curvaceous. Beautiful.

Jean sat near me in geometry class and was unable to do the work. Not all that good at the subject myself (but passing), I vowed silently to save her. Mustering courage—being next to any pretty girl transformed me into rubber—I volunteered to help her. Mrs. Scherrien, the nastiest woman I'd ever met and likely ever will meet, had just broadcasted our futures. In her repulsive stentorian hawkish croaking, she had proclaimed that two days hence we'd be examined on bisecting angles; our scores would count for 60% of the term grade.

Jean practically cried. I wanted to be her comforter and rescuer. We'd had a hello-how-are-you relationship, though, unbeknownst to her, I longed for more. "Don't worry," I said, "I can show you how to bisect."

Arranging to meet at her house after school, I felt, as our rendezvous drew near, weak in the knees, butterflies in the stomach, and dry in the mouth. Despite my malaise, I was joyous: Could our meeting be the start of our future? Would she see the me I saw, the me beyond the flesh? Fearful but hopeful, I went to her house and, feigning competence, tutored her.

Sucking in my stomach the two hours there and always facing her so she couldn't see the large folds framing my spongy backside, I felt fat. And I shuddered that she too would regard me that way. If she did (she must have), to her credit she never let on. Her manner and speech were kind and accepting, and sitting next to her at her kitchen table, my crush on her swelled.

When we finished the study session, I eagerly offered to repeat it the next day. She declined. Unaware of my disappointment, she said I'd already helped her and was "wonderful" for doing so. At that moment, I knew first love's confusion, for I was hopeful at hearing the compliment while downtrodden at feeling the rebuff.

My confusion disappeared the afternoon of the next day. Any hope I had had that there could be something deeper between us vanished as I saw her walking hand-in-hand with Harper Carter, a handsome boy my age but 50 pounds lighter, 10 inches at the waist smaller, and free of love-handles. I hated Harper Carter.

I stayed home my fifteenth summer finding relief in television and food. The outside was still antifat with striking vengeance, and I was still fat with striking visibility. Teachers and peers loathed my shape. I continued to accept their views as the only ones possible. Yet, by now, my proximity to my own fatness at least made me more tolerant of it.

Michael goes on to say what food meant to him at this time in his life: it was his pleasure, it was his pain, it was his salve.

Eating was the most fun on Sunday. Brunch could be lox and bagels, salami and eggs, kippers, bacon, ham, and toast with butter . . . all washed down with skim milk. (The nonfat milk was a bid for lower calories; at least we felt we had something lower in calories and were better for it.) Our home, like our food, was kept perfect in every way. To get up after watching television, I had to peel my fat legs off the plastic covers on the living room sofa.

Dinners during the workweek never equaled the mid-Sunday grandeur. But, as I have since learned, they also verged on the superior—meat (brisket), never less than two cooked vegetables (cooked with lots of butter and love), some raw carrots and celery (but who wanted them?), potatoes fried crisply, sometimes rice, sometimes both. Pie for afterwards, never naked on the plate, was dressed in ice cream (ice milk once in awhile because it sounded low-cal). The food parade never ended.

Even television and its companion the TV tray could not halt it. We usually sat down at six o'clock and began eating when we saw our filled plates. I always ate all of the visible reasons on mine to continue eating—when the food vanished, I stopped to refill, or just stopped. Rarely was I just satisfied, never was I left hungry. To be full was to be bloated.

Indeed, during my childhood and adolescence, food was love, and eating was ecstasy. Food, concern, and affection played on the same stage before the same audience of six who applauded and gave every indication that repeat performances would be highly approved of. Food, the great performer, could even boast a special holiday show.

Sometimes friends and relatives hosted food extravaganzas and rewarded you for feats of consumption. Once I went with my family to a party where fried chicken lay beside an array of side dishes and desserts and after-dessert temptations, all on a table inviting you to gorge. I did. Guests applauded the "healthiness" of my appetite. I deserved the approbation. I performed well.

Yet eating had its drawbacks, too. Often my sister was reproached for hiding cookies, though she always claimed to be innocent. My family touted antifat propaganda as much as anyone could. My grandparents and parents, degraders of fatness, warned that corpulence, ugliness, and weakness shared the same seat at the dinner table.

But we united in our common affliction. On those glorious Sundays, I frequently tried on my father's pants and came downstairs for approving laughter, which I learned to love. I was nearly his height, but he was king in the waistline. I kept getting closer, however, to dethroning him.

Society says don't be fat. Failing to heed this law means rejection. I still hear the warning "be's": be thin, be coordinated, be strong. And I still hear the important "have": have willpower. But little is ever within reach that tells me how to be thin, coordinated, and strong, or where to find willpower and how to boost it. The rebukes cry out louder than the remedies.

I still feel distance from others. I walk around them, not toward them. The fringes of my world are my world. My pain and my pleasure are alike, for I hate to be noticed while I long to be accepted. But the eyes that watch me sting.

As a child and teenager, from the many whom I touched, I learned that I was grotesque, actually burlesque. I came to believe that my body was afflicted. Yet, unlike the bent limb, the marked face, or the twisted frame, this affliction was a crime. And I was the criminal. Condemned by a jury of my peers, I was indicted as weak. They said I caused my burden, and because I did, I legitimized their abuse. I had a scar I was blamed for.[5]

Michael's recollections are of a time long past, but much of what he remembers is reality for many of today's overweight teenagers. True now as then is that the environment is decidedly antifat. It overflows with adults, adolescents, and children who decry obesity loudly and venomously.

MARGARET

Margaret is 16 and has two older brothers and one younger sister—each thin. As well, both her mother and father, stylishly thin, boast they weigh the same as they did on their graduating college. Only Margaret in this closely knit family of six is overweight, 60 pounds overweight. This status, as Margaret describes, is not pleasant.

> I hate being overweight. Worse, I hate being overweight when everyone else you're with isn't.
>
> Two summers ago, this all-alone feeling hit me and floored me. My family and I drove to Salt Lake City, Utah, to visit Aunt Ronda, Uncle Bill, and (their children) my cousins Eli, Isac, and Gabby. At the time, they were all bean poles. I weighed more than everyone except Dad and Uncle Bill. Tall and strong, they looked powerful more than overweight.
>
> My cousins loved to eat at a local mile-high sandwich spot, "The Grub Stake." Its walls pictured gold miners, mining pans, campfires, covered wagons, and women in bonnets—the Pioneer West of about 150 years ago. As you walked in, a tall young man wearing tight jeans, leather vest, scarf, cowboy boots, and ten-gallon hat took your name and assigned your group an Old West title like the tin-pans, the bar-keeps, the outlaws, or, as he labeled us, the nuggets—the 11 nuggets.

To the host's left stood an old-time, stand-up weight scale, the top of which housed a giant glass-encased circle of large black numbers from 0 to 250 and a skinny black needle. No way was I going to climb on the scale and advertise my weight. Or so I thought. The restaurant's policy was that each person eats for the menu price of her meal or for what she weighs—four or five cents per pound. My cousins, brothers, and sister eagerly jumped on the scale. My aunt, uncle, and parents refused to weigh in, either because they believed the menu cost was cheaper or most likely because they didn't want to broadcast their pounds. Why then they made me weigh in, I'll never know.

It was unfair, silly, and cruel. For what I'd eat—maybe they thought I could finish a cow—the menu price was plainly cheaper. But they insisted so loudly, I stepped on the device, embarrassed.

I closed my eyes for a second, hoping the thing was broken—wouldn't work or would weigh me low—and praying no one else in the restaurant could see what it'd show. As the long needle swung far around, I knew my hopes were quashed. And, as the phony cowboy host loudly announced just before his mouth widened into a grin, "Guess you'd better not pay her weight if you all want to eat," I knew my prayers were unheard.

I couldn't believe the guy had said that. I couldn't believe my family had laughed when he did. I laughed loudly, too, but boiled inside.

Margaret goes on to describe what she believes others believe about her eating.

This year we had Thanksgiving. All of the family that lives in town (my four grandparents, three uncles, four aunts, and six cousins) came for the annual binge. I love most of them but hate when any of them eat with us; I feel like I'm on display.

They think all the overweight overeat. Maybe I'm wrong, but I think they hate to see heavy people eat, especially me. I'm supposed to exist on air, only. This Thanksgiving, I promised myself not to eat, to show them I'm no pig. I planned to have a small meal after they had gone.

The dining room table was a picture of overabundance. On it lay every Thanksgiving dish imaginable, and a few that aren't in the books. Besides the huge turkey, there were raisin muffins, dishes of sage stuffing, apple stuffing, squash pie, candied yams, cooked carrots in syrup, cranberry, and five different desserts—four my relatives had brought, one (pumpkin pie) I had made.

I munched on a few carrots and celery sticks from the kitchen and allowed myself one small slice of turkey—white meat. Finally, after several hours everyone left, stuffed. Now it was time for me. But instead of having the small tastes of stuffing, turkey, and pumpkin pie I had promised myself, I really ate. I felt deprived, noticed (not for control but for dieting), and angry for earlier denial. Why should I have denied myself? I had three helpings of everything.

Several times, Margaret has tried to diet, but each time her dieting has been extreme, disappointing, and damning to her sense of self-worth. Once, in desperation to reduce, she tried the half-day-fast, regular-dinner routine, only to find that it made her eat more than usual.

I decided to take off 30 pounds. I thought the quicker it goes, the better I'd feel. I didn't tell anyone what I'd planned, figuring the fewer who knew, the easier it'd be. I'd heard on TV about liquid diets—drink your food, and then eat a regular dinner. I thought I'd cut out everything but the dinner.

On the first day of my new torture, after awakening and getting dressed for school, I had a glass of water; that's all. Nobody at home said I should eat. For lunch at school, I had more water, and when I came home, another drink of it. For dinner, I ate a lettuce salad without dressing, three slices of roast beef, and a baked potato. No seconds, no dessert, no snacks.

I lasted two days. Either I was ill (usually a headache) or hungry all of the time. I was so famished the second day that at 4:30 p.m., instead of the water alone I had 18 cookies, five fingerfuls of peanut butter, and two slices of bread with butter and jam. I felt powerless, trapped, and doomed.

As you will read, schemes to lose weight fast and on your own likely will harm more than help. Also, as you will learn, food plans that restrict too much, that force giving up too much, often give out. Chances are you will punish yourself when they end. And, if they last too long, chances are you will have problems far worse than owning extra pounds.

Margaret continues her description, focusing now on what she faces at home.

Meals with the family are the worst time. I feel that if I eat like Julie, Doug, and Donnie, I'll hear something about being too heavy.

I was about 10 when my brothers first called me "Fatso" and meant it. I really hate that word. "Fat" means ugly and weak and useless. If you're fat, everyone thinks you're powerless, have no control.

Mom thinks that dinner is a meal you must have to be healthy. When I was 10 and younger, if I left anything on my plate I got told, "Don't you care that there are starving people? They'd love what you get for free." Also, she'd say, "No dessert, if you don't clean your plate." Then, a few hours or days later, she and Dad would say, "The reason you're getting chubby (another word I hate) is because you eat too many sweets."

Telling me to eat everything to get dessert and then saying I shouldn't eat so many sweet things is inconsistent.

Sometimes my parents are ashamed of me. I get good grades, but they want me looking slim, too. Maybe they feel that I'm overweight because of something they did or didn't do.

School is also a problem for Margaret, as she explains.

I first remember overweight being an issue at school when I was in Mrs. Pirie's sixth grade class. I wasn't gross, or anything like that, but I was definitely heavy. Mrs. Pirie was nice and never made me feel bad. She never told weight jokes. Some of the kids did, even Kathy, who had been my best friend since third grade. Kathy and I still did things together and talked on the phone at night, but everything was different that year. She seemed embarrassed by our friendship. Marla was the most popular girl in the sixth grade and made more fun of my body than did anyone else. Kathy wanted Marla to like her, so I guess Kathy had to tone down her friendship with me.

Marla seemed to hate anyone who was heavy. She wanted to fight me. I was scared, but nothing except shoving ever occurred.

As I became more and more overweight, school became more and more horrible. Tenth grade was the worst. By that time Kathy had moved to Pittsburgh, and I had few friends, no best friend.

I'm now a junior in high school, and although I don't feel I'm going to be someone's punching bag I don't feel desirable either. I'm friends with Joe, but he likes Cheryl. I'm not close to any other boy. Mom and Dad have these friends who know some boy my age. They all tried to get him to take me to one of his school dances. Big mistake. Coming over my house to meet me (I felt like a piece of meat), he left soon; he never did call to ask me out. Even though that hurt, I'm glad he didn't—not my type. I don't think my parents will try that again.

Finding clothes to fit is impossible. I have tent-size garments and many loose-fitting over-blouses in my closet. Loose is the operative word. I look for clothes that hide my shape, but they make me huge. The clothes the thin girls wear are forbidden to me, another difference I hate.

And sales clerks don't want my business; they're rude. They make me feel that my heaviness creates hassles for them and that if I wasn't weak, they wouldn't have the hassles.

Few female film and TV stars are fat. Those who are I like because everywhere I go, every magazine I read, every movie I watch, beauty begins with a "T." It shouldn't be that way.

Although their ages, sexes, and experiences differ, Michael and Margaret share common ground: each has felt the sting of the antifat; each has been accused of being responsible for and deserving of society's indignation and condemnation.

You may see similarities between you and Michael or Margaret or feel no kinship whatsoever with them. In either case, I hope you find the pages that follow informative and useful. They tell about overweight and what to do and not do about it.

WORDS

Sticks and stones break bones but names don't hurt. Nonsense. Whoever penned that old saw was never labeled "fat ass," "fat s---," "fat f---," "porker," "fatso," "blimp," "chubby cheeks," or "lard butt." Names can pain. They are nails the antifat drive into sensitive flesh. Both Michael and Margaret would proclaim loudly and clearly, names can hurt.

Once I asked a young teenage patient of mine if she thought of herself as fat. Glaring at me as if I had sinned, she said, "Fat is a dirty word." For her, as for Michael and for Margaret, the word "fat" has meanings beyond what the dictionary reveals; it carries the excess baggage of worthless, weak, ugly. When I use it, I mean only extra tissue on the body medically and commonly called "fat." Never do I intend to insult.

The teenage years are a time of discovery, development, and change. If you are overweight, they could also be a time of having a scar you are blamed for. Let us now find out more about that scar.

THE SCAR —————————————————

Teenage obesity is on the upswing. Scrutinizing information from the National Health and Examination Surveys, Tufts University researcher Dr. Dietz and his associates show that obesity is up by 39% among those 12- to 17-year-olds who are fatter than 85% of their peers. For those even fatter, fatter than 95% of their peers, obesity is up by 64%.[1] These trends are most pronounced for teenage girls.

More and more teenagers are getting more and more obese because of what they eat, how they play, and how they get from place to place. Can you go more than a couple of blocks without seeing a tempting doughnut shop, bakery, or fast-food restaurant? Everywhere, there are places to eat. Everywhere, there are calorie-rich, often fatty, foods to choose. Everywhere, there are televisions, movie theaters, and captivating sit-down games to enjoy. Everywhere, there are cars and buses to get to these places.

The question remains, though, why one teenager gets obese and another, who eats and exercises like him or her, does not. The answer may involve heredity.

THE GENETIC CONNECTION

You were born after developing trillions of cells, each with 46 chromosomes—23 from each parent, 23 pairs.

Chromosomes carry hundreds to thousands of genes, determining whether you are blonde, brunette, or a redhead; whether you have blue, hazel, or brown eyes; whether you have ten fingers, ten toes or eight fingers, eight toes; whether you have black, brown, or white skin; and whether you are a candidate for Huntington's chorea, heart disease, or sickle-cell anemia. You are programmed early. And obesity may be in your program.

Heredity influences weight and amount of fat. Twins coming from the same fertilized ovum, alike genetically, are more apt to weigh the same than are twins coming from different fertilized ova. And this is so, psychiatrist Dr. Albert Stunkard of the University of Pennsylvania indicates, for twins reared under the same roof or, the more exacting comparison, for twins reared under different roofs.

What's more, heredity (nature) figures into the obesity story when the weights and heights of adoptees are compared with those of their biologic and adoptive parents. To show this, Dr. Stunkard and his associates, using the Danish Adoption Register, secured records on more than 3500 adoptees living in Copenhagen.[2] From this group, they selected 540 men and women of middle age. Stunkard found that sons and daughters were more like their biologic parents.

Genes affect obesity, but they affect it differently from how they influence hair color, eye color, and skin color, and differently from how they influence the slope of the eyelids or hairiness of the legs. Whether you will see the world through blue or brown eyes and walk on it with black or white legs is determined soon after conception. It is set. What happens in your home or in your mind or in your school does not change what is determined.

Obesity is not determined, it is influenced. What happens to you as you live impacts whether you become overweight. Dr. Stunkard explains:

> Obesity is not determined at conception. What is inherited is a liability that requires a suitable environment in order to be manifested. (p. 212)[3]

Predisposed is not predestined. There may be a violin virtuoso within you, but you will need violin lessons before appearing on stage at Carnegie Hall. You may be able to run like a gazelle or have the strength of two men, but you will need training before competing in sprints or lifts at the Olympics. Talents, like flowers, need nurturing before blossoming. Genes and environment (nature and nurture) interact, each influencing your becoming and staying overweight. Genes do not doom to lifelong obesity. They set the stage, but you and your world have starring roles.

YOUR THREE SIDES

Imagine you have three sides: a body side, an energy side, a behavior side. And imagine each side has two or more parts to it: The body side includes weight, fat, height, health, and more; the energy side includes calorie intake and calorie outgo; the behavior side includes eating, moving, contradictions, planning, thinking.

Figure 2.1 depicts this as a triangle. Arrows on the triangle mean that different parts at different sides affect one another to fatten you or to slim you. Behavior affects calories—the amount consumed, the amount expended. And the balance over time of calories taken in and burned up affects body—how much you weigh, how fat you are.

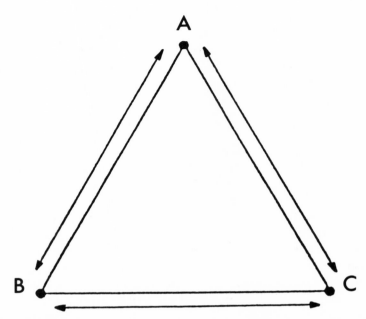

FIGURE 2.1. Your three sides. (A) *Body side:* weight, fat, height, percent overweight, blood pressure, plasma lipid levels, glucose tolerance, fitness. (B) *Behavior side:* eating, activity, contradictory messages, self-statements, plan violations. (C) *Energy side:* calorie intake, calorie outgo.

Body

As shown, there are a wealth of entries at this side of the triangle. We will discuss most of them in the ensuing pages.

Fat

With its televisions, tabloids, billboards, and movies, our thin-crazy culture likens fat to pestilence, ugliness, and disease. So even at tender ages, many of us become haters of fat, fearers of fat, defilers of fat. Preteen and teenage girls, particularly but not exclusively, dread it. They worry, indeed panic, that if their obesity shows they will be shamed and shunned, and as a result they diet—some emaciate, some cycle binging with purging.

But we all need fat. Born with it, we would perish without it. Dr. Pauline Powers of the University of South Florida College of Medicine teaches that of the ways the body holds energy, storing fat is the most efficient, for storing carbohydrate means also storing water.[4] If carbohydrate fueled all of our activities, we would be waterlogged and ponderous.

Fat is fuel to empower, to survive. When a newborn, you were about 12% fat. By the toddler stage, you likely were twice that fat but then probably slimmed down. At puberty and if female, you through nature became fatter than the boy down the road.

Suppose now, 32% of you is fat. If 16 years old and that fat, you are too fat. If you are 190 pounds, the nearly 61 pounds of you that is fat (190 × 0.32) would be stored as triglyceride (glycerol joined to three fatty acids) in fat cells.

Fat Cells

Being 16 and 32% fat, you could have billions upon billions of fat cells, having been born with about five or six billion of them, says Joseph Wilkinson in his book *Don't Raise Your Child to be a Fat Adult*. An adult with an obesity condition could have over 100 billion.[5] Think of fat cells as depots for fat—storage bins for fat. These depots may increase in size (hypertrophy) or in number (hyperplasia); size increases may trigger number increases as fat-cell size crosses some threshold and obesity becomes pronounced.

Years ago, a popular theory said that the young and overweight were headed toward adult years of unmanageable, unremitting obesity if they overate at the wrong times during development because doing so increased their numbers of fat cells. And once there, fat cells stayed. The idea was that, compared with adults who fatten during adulthood, young people who fatten when young and grow up to become corpulent adults would have greater than normal numbers of fat cells. Adults who fatten as adults would show mainly enlarged fat cells. Before weight loss, fat cells are there, filled with triglyceride. After weight loss, they are still there, but shrunken. Possibly, when shrunken, fat cells signal the owner to fill them up, to eat and fatten.

If you want to stay thin, according to theory, too many fat cells means too many problems. When the young owner of the excess fat cells becomes an adult and wants to slim, she will have to starve herself to stay thin. The body fights the efforts to keep it thin and wins. Sick of continual hunger and tired of the psychological upset it brings, the dieter stops dieting. And, as Dr. Richard Nisbett of the University of Michigan argues, obesity returns.

That fat cells do not go away, and that so many of them can appear before and during the teen years, causes some scientists and practitioners to call for early treatment—stop fat cells from multiplying. Safely ending the fat cell proliferation makes sense. But not all obese untreated teenagers face relentless adult obesity.

Energy

This side of the triangle has two parts, calorie intake and calorie outgo.

Long ago, the late Ronald Deutsch, a highly respected nutrition writer, discriminated energy from vigor.[6] He noted that vigor (supported by good health from good nutrition) allows one to play sports, keep late hours, and hold a part-time job. Energy, a scientific term, means fuel from food and is written as calories. Perhaps to you, calories are hobgoblins that ruin the enjoyment the food gives. Perhaps to you, calories exact a price for pleasure: The more the fun, the more the calories, the more the suffering.

But do not think of calories as microscopic evildoers hiding in cakes, cookies, hot dogs, croissants, buttery bagels, and the like. Calories are in chemical bonds, and when your body breaks down these bonds in food, energy is released.

The energy, written as calories, is heat. A calorie multiplied by 1000 is a kilocalorie, usually called Calorie. A Calorie is the heat needed to warm one kilogram of water one degree centigrade—from approximately 15 to 16 degrees centigrade. In modern nutrition books, you will see the word "joules." Joules or kilojoules, today's way of talking about food energy, are smaller measures than are kilocalories—it takes almost 4.2 kilojoules to equal 1 kilocalorie. A 500-kilocalorie hunk of dark chocolate approximates 2100 kilojoules. Henceforward, for clarity, I will describe energy as "calories" and mean by that word, kilocalories.

Balancing and Imbalancing Energy

Type and amount of food consumed determine amount of calories available. You are a 15-year-old, 5 foot 4 inch, 125-pound girl who has eaten five meals during the day—two snacks plus breakfast, lunch, and dinner. Suppose your day's intake equals 2200 calories, the recommended energy intake for someone your age, sex, weight, and height. (Compare this with the allowances for 15-year-old boys.) Table 2.1, from the National Research Council's Recommended Dietary Allowances, provides a current listing of energy recommendations.[7] To arrive at them, the makers of this table have considered age, sex, weight, height, and activity. The last column, average energy allowance daily, will concern you more than will the others. (Note: What is best for you may be more or less than what is listed there.)

It matters from where calories come. Protein contributes about 4 calories per gram, carbohydrate about 4 calories per gram, and fat more than 9 calories per gram. Suppose today you get nearly three-fourths of your calories from ladles of gravy dousing your hefty orders of french fries, from bowls of extra-rich ice cream, from dozens of cashews, and from tablespoons of peanut butter. Tomorrow, you will take in the same number of calories, but will not have any of these fatty foods. Instead, you will eat vegetable-bake and other low-in-fat items. Today's diet is high fat, tomorrow's will not be.

The difference affects you because calories from the nutrient of fat add disproportionately to getting fat. Fat not only yields many calories—more than twice as many gram for gram as the other two nutrients—but calories from fat also seem to fatten more easily (see Chapter 3).

The number of calories burned is determined by the energy used to stay alive and grow, the energy used to move about and recreate, and the energy used to deal with the foods eaten, called the thermic effect. Let's say you are moderately active and play badminton and volleyball frequently. Yesterday, you consumed and expended about 2200 calories; intake and outgo of energy balanced.

If instead imbalance occurred, it could mean you took in *more* calories than you used up. Continued and prolonged imbalance fattens—on average, a 3500-calorie surplus adds one pound of extra fat. This surplus forms when you overeat or your body is unusually efficient at capturing and storing nutrients from foods, or when you move too little, or when all of these events happen.

Imbalance could also mean you took in *fewer* calories than you expended. You created not a surplus but a deficit by lowering calorie intake, or by raising calorie outgo, or by doing both. Imbalance that causes a calorie deficit reduces fat. Teenagers favor lowering calorie intake to create the calorie deficit, but by itself such lowering is not the best way to create it.

Involuntary Calorie Outgo and Life

You need energy to pump blood, to breathe, to digest food—to do the involuntary acts of living. The energy it takes for them accounts for the largest drain on energy reserves. Indeed, involuntary calorie outgo over the decades of life is a river of energy compared with the brook of it used to walk, run, and play.

Energy has been your life-force since birth and will not stop serving you until death. The estimate of it, in calories per day, is called resting energy expenditure (REE); it is the seventh column of Table 2.1. When reading books and articles on nutrition and energy, you might see involuntary energy spending referred to as basal metabolic rate

TABLE 2.1. Median Heights and Weights and Recommended Energy Intake[a]

Category	Age (years) or condition	Weight		Height		REE[b] (kcal/ day)	Average energy allowance (kcal)[c]		
		kg	lb	cm	in		Multiples of REE	Per kg	Per day[d]
Infants	0.0–0.5	6	13	60	24	320		108	650
	0.5–1.0	9	20	71	28	500		98	850
Children	1–3	13	29	90	35	740		102	1300
	4–6	20	44	112	44	950		90	1800
	7–10	28	62	132	52	1130		70	2000
Males	11–14	45	99	157	62	1440	1.70	55	2500
	15–18	66	145	176	69	1760	1.67	45	3000
	19–24	72	160	177	70	1780	1.67	40	2900
	25–50	79	174	176	70	1800	1.60	37	2900
	51+	77	170	173	68	1530	1.50	30	2300

Females								
	11–14	46	101	157	62	1310	1.67	47	2200
	15–18	55	120	163	64	1370	1.60	40	2200
	19–24	58	128	164	65	1350	1.60	38	2200
	25–50	63	138	163	64	1380	1.55	36	2200
	51+	65	143	160	63	1280	1.50	30	1900
Pregnant	1st trimester								+0
	2nd trimester								+300
	3rd trimester								+300
Lactating	1st 6 months								+500
	2nd 6 months								+500

[a] Modified from National Research Council. (1989). *Recommended Dietary Allowances* (10th ed.). Washington, DC: National Academy Press.
[b] Calculation based on FAO equations (Table 3–1 of Ref. 7), then rounded.
[c] In the range of light to moderate activity, the coefficient of variations is ± 20%.
[d] Figure is rounded.

(BMR). The REE and BMR differ by less than 10% and mean energy expended at rest.

Voluntary Calorie Outgo and Life

Take out the garbage, walk from the living room to the front door, do the wash, iron wrinkled pants, wash your face. These activities, day-to-day routines, do not wind you; they burn calories above what would be used for sleeping. Instead, walk a mile or two, or slow-jog without becoming breathless or exhausted. These activities are probably aerobic for you. They are fueled mainly by fat, can last for a long time, can be done while conversing with someone nearby, and improve the ability to use oxygen.

Sprint 100 yards, or for a few minutes run quickly to score during tennis or racquetball, or speed down the football field. These intense and fatiguing activities, called anaerobic, are fueled mainly by carbohydrate stores and cannot be continued for long.

During any day, you are likely to do routines, aerobics, and anaerobics, alternating among them. Each serves you well. To lessen overweight, most programs emphasize routines and aerobics.

Even though the total energy used by voluntary activity is usually much less than that used by involuntary activity, voluntary activity accounts for enough to help you thin. Benefits of becoming a mover include:

- Reducing fat
- Staying lean
- Contouring the body
- Increasing fitness
- Taking the burden off changing intake as *the* vehicle to control overweight

- Improving health
- Enhancing feelings of mastery and pleasure
  Helping maintain progress at controlling over-
  weight
- Helping maintain predieting metabolic rates

About this last plus, dieting (especially restrictive dieting) can lower metabolic rate, making it harder to continue losing pounds and inches. When you diet, your body adapts to less food—less energy in, less energy out—and as a result, you need fewer calories to live. With fewer calories needed, you will find it harder to create and sustain the deficit of calories you must create and sustain to get rid of extra fat. Reducing gets tougher. In *Living Without Dieting*, Drs. John Foreyt and Ken Goodrick, psychologists at Baylor College of Medicine in Texas, say that exercise may help to lessen or reverse this disruptive drop in metabolic rate.[8] Strive for the active life.

Behavior

When you knock on a door, you behave. When you kick it in, you behave. When you walk, talk, smile, grin, scratch, hold, push, shove, embrace, condemn, argue, advise, or think, you behave. Be it good or bad or neutral, be it fun or boring or painful, be it proper or improper, be it sinful or virtuous, behavior is action.

You go to Aunt Willa's $7-a-person All-You-Can-Stuff Food Emporium, and Aunt Willa prays she never sees you again. At the end of your first trip to the steam table, you return to your booth with five drumsticks, a side of pork spareribs, fried onion rings, macaroni salad, and corn-on-the-cob dripping butter. Hearty and hale, but no longer hungry, you reenter the cafeteria line to get apple pie, pecan pie, and cherry pie. Throughout the meal, you fill and refill your 14-ounce glass with popular colas.

Eating and drinking at Aunt Willa's are behaviors that affect calorie balance. So does going to the school track and running one mile a day. Eating and exercising are actions that balance and imbalance calories, and they (as do other behaviors) allow you a door into the obesity triangle. Let's now look at a most perplexing behavior at that door.

Contradictions

What others close to you say and do about your being overweight can be confusing. At the Manitoba Obesity Clinic, our patients tell us about these inconsistencies.

Eat to Be a Friend, but Friends Aren't Overweight. Here, social eating runs up against becoming or remaining thin (see the example of Alycen in Chapter 6). An overweight teenager who joins friends at a local coffeeshop or fast-food restaurant must decide whether to eat there. If he acts like his chums, he conforms to the first part of the message—he eats to be sociable. But by so doing, he increases the risk of violating the second part of it—being overweight. As well, he chances teasing for being an eater who is heavy. If he chooses not to eat anything, he in effect says something is wrong with him. He not only violates the first part of the message, does not eat, but he also says, by his actions, that he is overweight, calling into question his status as a friend. Besides, if he eats little or nothing there, he may be tormented for being an overweight dieter. If he avoids such get-togethers, he excludes himself from many social plans. Damned at every turn, he may retreat into high-calorie, high-fat solitary eating, widening the chasm separating him from his friends.

Food Is Splendor, but Overweight Is Ugly. When telling of the superior meals he received and the antifat messages he heard, Michael recounted this contradiction (Chapter 1). At home he witnessed not a two-sided statement but a discordance between deeds and words. Michael and his family condoned, even encouraged, irresistible displays of rich tasty food while they condemned overweight. Michael loved the actions that made less than plenty insufficient but loathed the words that made overweight a crime.

Play Sports with Us to Be One of Us, but We Have No Time for the Overweight Who Play Badly. Michael describes this contradiction when he writes of his junior high and high school athletic nightmares. And he tells how he solved these dilemmas: getting excused from gym class. But, as he also points out, the solution had a price tag: increasing the distance he felt from his peers.

Often, to be accepted, one must play sports. But if thought bad at them, one loses opportunities to acquire skills needed to be good at them. One without what it takes cannot get what it takes because of not having what it takes. Confusing logic!

Banishment from team sports soon fulfills the prophecy of being too poor at them to play them. Many overweight teenagers have no access to team sports because coaches or team captains believe that the overweight cannot possibly do well. If given the opportunity to play, it is as a shock absorber or battering ram. Ridicule on and off the field ends in avoidance and further rejection.

Clean Your Plate If You Want Dessert, but Stop Eating So Many Sweets. This double message is probably in your past. Believing in your needing a balanced dinner, despising your appearing to waste food, and disliking your being overweight, parents conveyed it. They told you if you would finish dinner, you would get dessert. But then later, if you complained of clothes being tight or if you voiced concern about overweight, they told you to eat fewer sweets. They condoned, even proffered, after-dinner sweets and later condemned your having had them. Inconsistent!

We have looked at teenage overweight and devised a triangle to organize some of the critical information about it. Next, we address dieting.

CHAPTER **3**

DIETING AND DANGER ————

Dieting: It helps, it hurts; it succeeds, it fails; it encourages, it frustrates; it gladdens, it saddens. Dieting is behavior that does different things to different people. Dieting is what the irascible feline Garfield so aptly and caustically likens to passing away, to "Die with a *T*."[1] Says Dr. Kelly Brownell of Yale University, each year diet food companies, diet book publishers, and diet drug manufacturers make millions upon millions of dollars helping you and others test the diet idea.[2] Dieters are young and old, male and female, fat and thin. Teens, especially girls, diet, and perhaps because they do, many are malnourished. Nutritionists Drs. Betty Kirkley at the University of North Carolina and Jean Burge at Ohio State University say:

> . . . teenage girls are the most poorly fed members of our society relative to their nutritional requirements. (p. 68)[3]

Each of you has reasons for cutting back on food: Maybe you hate the look of your body, maybe you fear getting fat, maybe both. One teen I know speaks graphically, "It's a meat market out there. If I look bad because I don't diet, I'll be history." If you hate your shape and fear what eating more will do to it, you are listening to what society says is attractive and sexy. Everywhere such "shape" news bombards you—on billboards, on television, in movies, in magazines; there is no escape.

But the years change the messages, especially those for females. When told, "Don't be fat," you are told things your mother heard, but not as strictly. As Dr. David Garner and his colleagues make clear, today's "beautiful" young woman is thinner than her counterpart of years ago.[4] Yet, the teenage female of now is fatter than the teenage female of yesterday. So, teens of the 1990s are under fire: They are fatter than teens of a few decades ago and are told to be thinner than were the glamorous of a few decades ago. The rules of the beauty game have changed, for the worse.

It is tougher to compete and, as a result, some adolescent girls terrified of becoming fat want to lose weight even if already thin, a problem we will soon discuss. What's more, some of the overweight, those feeling far behind in the race for beauty and acceptance, want to lose far too much. Life is easier for boys, yet it is miles from easy.

Usually diets last for a year, a month, a week, or a day. Though to some they seem never to end, dieting for most is temporary. You go on a diet, you go off a diet. But dieting in this sense is troublesome, for it says do something and then stop doing it. The unfulfilled promise: Changes last even after you stop the diet. The upsetting oversight: Return to ways that abetted getting fat in the first place—high-fat eating accompanied by day after day of sit-down games and car rides instead of active games and walking—and you will again fatten.

Here are some dieting don'ts.

DON'T FAST

Fasting deprives totally. Drs. George Blackburn and Konstantin Pavlou, nutrition researchers at Harvard University, say this hunger strike may cause nausea, dizziness, loss of minerals and muscle, and worse.[5] No one should fast without being under a physician's care, and even that guarantees little.

Just because the needle on the scale drops during a fast does not mean what is lost is all fat. Nutritionist Jane Rees of the University of Washington calls starvation and semistarvation, and the body's natural fight against these two self-inflicted tortures, self-defeating.[6] Warn Drs. John Foreyt and Ken Goodrick of Baylor, don't starve or lower calories so restrictively that you are continually hungry.[7]

DON'T SKIP MEALS

Favorites to skip are breakfast and lunch. Leaving for school without eating and then, compounding the crime, denying yourself lunch fans your smoldering hunger into a raging inferno of want. After school, before dinner, you will likely extinguish it with rich snacks and drinks, devouring the first, second, and third sweets staring at you from the refrigerator—the cheesecake, the cherry pie, the cola.

DON'T TRY TO SHRINK YOUR APPETITE CHEMICALLY

Relying on a diet potion or pill to curb appetite controls weight passively. Taking the chemical says, "I have no control, so I'll let chemistry do the work." But you do have control. Sometimes, though, the control seems hidden, and you have to search for it. If you think you are weaker than a feather against a strong wind, build control; use the principles and tactics of this book.

Also, refuse over-the-counter preparations for losing weight because, not only don't many work, but also, warns Dr. Faith Fitzgerald of the University of California Davis Medical Center, many contain phenylpropanolamine, a potentially harmful drug often found in cold remedies:

> While it has no proven efficacy in causing sustained weight reduction, phenylpropanolamine has been implicated in the induction of hypertension, arrhythmias ... and severe CNS (central nervous system) toxicity. (p. 233)[8]

Diet-pill risks outweigh diet-pill benefits.

DON'T SUCCUMB TO FAD DIETING

Cashing in on the desperation of many of us to be thin, diet-hucksters greedily and cruelly—eyes on profits, minds off principles—conjure deceit and foolishness. They build fad diets. Promising to turn fantasy into reality, these wizards of diet vow their results will surpass your dreams and eclipse the claims of experts. The wizards' nostrums are in popular magazines, tabloids, and newspapers. They are usually endorsed by a celebrity, says Dr. Fitzgerald, or by some satisfied customer declaring the remedy holds "the secret for success." Says the promoter, the diet with its special elixir or foods is yours ... for a price. Referring to such "magic" diets, Harvard Drs. Blackburn and Pavlou advise potential buyers to walk away.[9]

Most fad diets pledge the quick fix—"do what we say, flab melts away." Years ago, says science writer Gina Kolata, one product even claimed to *wash* fat away.[10]

Some fad diets ask you to eliminate essential nutrients like carbohydrate. And some dwell on the pluses of a certain food: the grapefruit diet, the hot dog diet. Some fad diets do more than rob you, bore you, or insult you, though. They sicken you, possibly kill you. In *A Diet for Living*, highly respected nutritionist Dr. Jean Mayer says one of the most dangerous, unwise, unproductive, and deadly is the macrobiotic diet, promoted by Sakurazawa Nyoiti, more commonly known as George Ohsawa.[11] This diet gradually, painstakingly has you stop eating all foods except brown rice.

DON'T DENY YOURSELF EXCESSIVELY

Many teens find it difficult to work even seemingly normal diets because, impatient for results, they fall victim to the "more is better" fallacy: If cutting down *somewhat* is good, cutting down *more* is better.

Fueling the fallacy is the hurry-up attitude of "I want change, and I want it fast." Impatience forecasts trouble, for stringent diets deprive you nutritionally, as Drs. Kirkley and Burge warn, often resulting in too little iron and too little calcium.[12] You need iron. If deficient in it, you will be inefficient at work and at play, feeling run down and tired even after sleep. You need calcium to help build strong bones and teeth, to help nerves and muscles work, to help blood clot. A less likely trouble, but possible for young teenagers too stringently restricting calories, is setting back normal growth.

Diets that excessively deny leave you hungry and wanting to quit them, and they set up binging as well as the cycle described next.

DON'T BECOME A YO-YO DIETER

Develop a manageable, livable diet. The livable diet helps achieve a personally acceptable and healthy level of fatness. Eat and exercise rationally, healthfully. I will talk more of sensible eating and activity later.

The livable regimen contrasts with one that promotes the despicable, discouraging, defeating pattern of yo-yo dieting: dieting restrictively, stopping the diet, dieting restrictively again, stopping the diet another time, dieting restrictively again, and so on. It is this on–off–on pattern of weight cycling, proclaim some authorities, that justifies never dieting. Get off the rollercoaster, say these experts; it is going nowhere. And, they continue, trying to thin by dieting is worse than not trying to thin at all because dieting, restrictive dieting, breeds weight cycling.

What happens to those who diet, stop dieting, diet again, stop again, diet again . . . what happens to weight cyclers? About a decade ago, Dr. Kelly Brownell of Yale University and colleagues attempted to answer.[13] They fed rats a fatty diet and then a balanced one. Subsequently, they refed the rats the fatty diet and later on again the balanced one followed once more by the fatty diet—two cycles of dieting and overeating, of taking off and putting on weight.

Each time the rats ate the high-fat chow they gained—became obese—and each time they had the balanced diet they lost to normal. But during the second cycle of dieting followed by overeating compared to the first cycle of it, the rats put back on faster what they had taken off. And during the second cycle compared to the first one, they took more time to relose what they had regained.

Said differently, regaining lost weight took the rats just over six weeks the first time—the first cycle. Regaining lost weight took them only a couple of weeks the second time—the second cycle. Regaining got easier.

Losing what they had gained from overeating took three weeks the first time, but over twice that the second time. Losing got harder.

In short, yo-yo dieting speeded up the process of adding weight and slowed down that of subtracting it . . . for rats.

What about people? Studies of weight cycling when humans do the eating and losing and eating, as Dr. Thomas Wadden and colleagues of the University of Pennsylvania reported, do not always find what Dr. Brownell and colleagues found when rats do the weight cycling. Of his own experiment (done on 50 overweight women), Dr. Wadden says this:

> Results of this study do not support . . . that weight cycling was associated with an impaired ability to lose weight. (p. 206S)[14]

But, as he and his associates speculate, maybe weight cycling hurts people the most not in making losing harder and harder but in making gaining easier and easier, although even then many persons, indicate Drs. Brownell and Judith Rodin of Yale, are probably unaffected.[15]

Or, as Dr. Judith Rodin and colleagues of Yale University suggest in their study of weight cycling in women, maybe the damage lies in the pattern of fatness weight cycling promotes.[16] That is, maybe the worst thing about weight cycling is the way it causes fat to distribute on the body.

Think of fat people and fruit, apples and pears. Some fat people resemble apples, and others pears. Those shaped like apples accumulate most of their fat around their waists; for each of the apples, the ratio of the circumference of the waist to the circumference of the hips (waist/hips) is close to 1 or higher than 1—middles are quite round.

Those shaped like pears accumulate most of their fat on their hips and thighs; for each of the pears, the ratio of waist to hips is decidedly lower than 1.

In adults, the apple pattern links up with risk signs, as Drs. Lapidus and Bengtsson and others caution, for heart disease, diabetes, and more ills.[17] The pear pattern appears to be less hazardous. Dr. Rodin found female weight-cyclers more likely to be apple forms, abdominally fat. The apple shape may too be a sign of danger for children and teens. Perhaps yo-yo dieting that starts in the teen years and that becomes a way of coping with food during the adult years harms physically in the way Dr. Rodin discusses.

And perhaps it harms psychologically, for after quitting a restrictive, depriving, hunger-keeping diet, a diet you must quit, you may feel so disgusted with yourself, so hateful toward yourself, that self-esteem dives down. Feeling like a failure destined to be forever fat, you may in time once more try to thin but go disastrous steps further: undergo the grave diet of the anorexic, do the stuff-and-purge dance of the bulimic.

DISORDERS OF EATING

The most recent *Diagnostic and Statistical Manual* of the American Psychiatric Association describes several eating disorders.[18] Those of infancy or early childhood include *pica* and *rumination disorder*. *Pica* refers to eating things of no nutritional value (e.g., cloth, paint, sand, hair, string, pebbles, plaster, animal excrement). *Rumination disorder of infancy* is repeatedly regurgitating partly digested food; there's no gaining or there's weight loss. Pica and rumination disorder afflict the very young. Teens and young adults are affected by *anorexia nervosa* and *bulimia nervosa* (and combinations of the two); with both, dieting goes haywire.

Anorexia

Jana, age 16, implies she is a city girl with finances who suffers from anorexia.

> There's only three of us [mother, father, Jana] in our four-bedroom house. I have a car, so getting from place to place is easy. Besides, buses and cabs are everywhere. When I was 10, I was pudgy, at least that's what my friends said; I agreed. I dieted in grade six and thinned down but by grade eight was pudgy again. In grade ten, I started another diet. I remember I had a tennis date with my best friend Julie, and Mom brought home a tennis outfit. It was black; I refused to put it on. "Why black?" I asked.
>
> "Because black makes you look thinner," Mom answered. "Don't argue. I know about colors and shapes."

I wore it, but felt stupid. Julie asked me if I was in mourning, and she giggled. That laugh did it. Then and there, I decided to lose weight—from my then 140 pounds to 110 pounds—and to thin my thighs. Of all of the parts of my body I disliked, I hated my thighs the most.

The easiest and fastest way for me to lose was skipping breakfast and lunch. Every morning I weighed myself, but even though the pounds melted away, I still felt fat. I began to jog five miles daily, not for fitness but for quicker losses. Once, 90 degrees and humid outside, I forced myself to run until I almost dropped. By the fourth mile, I was so thirsty, I thought unless I had some water I'd pass out. But I pushed on to finish the fifth. Because I'd sweated buckets, I thought mostly about weighing myself and seeing my all-time low weight. I wouldn't let myself near a glass of water until I weighed in, twice to make sure.

Although during all this time the pounds fell off me, my thighs actually seemed to grow rounder. Maybe they looked bigger because the rest of me was smaller.

Each lower weight became my "fat weight," the danger weight. I had to get below the new low to feel comfortable, yet since every low became a high weight I dare not exceed, I rarely felt contented as I lost and lost and lost. Soon, because I wanted to lose faster, I gave up dinner. It wasn't hard to no longer sit with my parents at dinner, because at least I didn't have to listen to their nagging me to eat more.

Hunger became my friendly foe. I didn't like wanting to eat, but I knew wanting meant I was getting thinner. I was hungry much of the time, but happy to be losing. It's my body, and I'll change it how I wish, I thought. I'd nibble on this and that throughout the day, up to 400 calories per day usually, and drink a lot of water; often I'd eat ice. I'd weigh myself after each nibble. When I got down to 90 pounds, I felt that I was the boss of me. Even then I believed that if I ate a full meal, just one, I'd be on my way to a black tennis outfit again ... no matter that I'd given up both tennis and my friendship with Julie.

Everyone said I looked like a skeleton. Mom tells me my chest was caved in and my hip bones stuck out. She also says that my fingers and toes were purple and that my eyes had that hollowness you see in the eyes of a starving child. She and Dad worried I was dying. I never worried about dying from being thin. To me, being fat was being dead. Besides, I didn't think I was a skeleton. My thighs still dominated my body.

When I reached the weight of my 80-year-old grandmother, 75 pounds, I began finding larger and larger clumps of hair in my comb and soft, fine baby hair growing on my arms. When I told Mom, she said "That's it. You're going to the doctor."

He asked me when I last had had my period, and I couldn't remember. After he pinched and poked and asked 4000 more questions, he said I had to go to the hospital. I stayed there about five months.

At first, they put a needle in my arm to feed me. I pulled it out, thinking they were plotting to make me fat. They put it back in. Finally, they pulled it out, when I agreed to eat solid food.

There were other girls like me on the ward. For eating and gaining, we got rewards like phone privileges, weekends home, and the freedom to walk on the hospital grounds (it was landscaped beautifully with roses, ferns, and oaks). But I hated being there. I agreed to work up to taking in over 2000 calories per day, and they promised to reward me for trying to and for adding ounces and pounds. All the girls on the ward ate together in the cafeteria. I know that some of them didn't really consume much but drank rivers of water to be heavier for the daily weight check.

My parents and I met every week with a staff counselor. I liked her because she didn't put all the blame on me for the eating problem or all the responsibility on me to get rid of it. We still meet weekly with her, though I'm no longer in the hospital. Funny, I feel that she's helped lift a weight off me as she's helped put weight on me. Each Saturday my parents and I go to the hospital, and before our sessions begin, I weigh in private and say what I'm doing to feel good about myself.

I still worry about getting fat, but I also don't want to get too thin. I eat three meals a day usually, but nobody forces me to or yells if one day I don't. My thighs are fat, but not that fat.

As Drs. David Schlundt of Vanderbilt University and William Johnson of the University of Mississippi School of Medicine write in *Eating Disorders,* Jana fits the picture of a restrictor-type anorexic. She starves (or did starve) herself, feeling hunger but avoiding food. Had she periodically stuffed and purged while she so severely dieted, she would be called a bulimic-type anorexic.[19]

All anorexics do not have exactly the same symptoms. But it is likely, says the American Psychiatric Association, that an anorexic will lose enough to be and stay at least 15% lighter than normal for her age and height. Or, if growing, she will fail to gain, so that she is 15% lighter than what she should weigh.

Even though underweight, she will be deathly afraid of getting fat. What's more, although quite skinny, she will feel fat and may pick a part of her body that "proves" (only to her) that she is fat—distorted body image. Finally, she will miss menstrual cycles—three misses in a row is diagnostic.

The teenage girl with anorexia may feel that she needs to be perfect. If she violates a self-imposed standard of excellence (perhaps a diet standard like no chocolate cookies ever again), she is sure she has done the unpardonable. She may be a diet expert having weight cycled often. She may have been overweight, but even if not, she is preoccupied with her weight. She may feel little control over her destiny, having demanding parents; only by rigidly dieting does she feel in command. She thinks about food much of the time and may be hungry most of the time—the term "anorexia, loss of appetite," is inaccurate.

Because of her ceaseless overly strict dieting, she may have an abnormally low heart rate, an abnormally low blood pressure, dry skin, and swelling. She may eventually possess baby-soft hair, lanugo, on her arms and legs. Also, because of inadequate nutrition, she may disturb the balance of her electrolytes—minerals (e.g., potassium, sodium, chloride) helping regulate the body's fluid balance, nervous system, and more. As a result of this imbalance, her heart may beat irregularly, and she may suffer cramps, dizzy periods, and fainting spells. She could die.

She may love to cook, but shun, her own meals. She may find it hard to sleep and painful to sit (no cushion of fat) and feel irritable much of the time. Because of impoverished stores of fat, she may be often cold. She may feel depressed or, because starvation causes release of endorphins (a natural opiate of the body), she may feel a sense of well-being as if nothing obstructs. She may keep to herself, shying away from past friends or from making new ones.

Above all, she preoccupies herself with thinning. She avidly seeks and finds what everyone except her is horrified to see: an emaciated replica of her former self. If treated, she can win the battle against anorexia. But even if a winner, she must remain wary of its return, for anorexia can come back and kill her.

I have used "she" in my descriptions because far more females than males are anorexic; yet, there are anorexic boys and men.

Bulimia

As well, far more females than males are bulimic, but unlike anorexics most bulimics hover near normal weight; a few become slightly overweight or underweight. The bulimic teenager binges and purges, stuffs and gets rid of what's stuffed. Her shape and weight are everything to her. Her fear of fat rises to an unbearable pitch during the aftermath of having yielded to the ruling impulse to gorge cakes, cookies, chips, dip, candy, nearly anything, sometimes even garbage. About this extreme, Drs. Schlundt and Johnson write of one young woman's demon:

> ... walk into a restaurant, sit down at a recently vacated table, and finish any food that was left on the plates. She also reported that the garbage dumpsters at certain restaurants were good places to find edible leftovers. (p. 90)[20]

Secretly, the bulimic may binge twice a week or many times a day, taking in hundreds to thousands of calories during each episode. When bingeing, she feels that eating is out of control. It is.

During a binge, she usually eats rapidly and voraciously, stopping only when there is stomach pain or discomfort, when out of food, or when interrupted. After the binge, she is desperate to purge. "If I don't lose the food now, it'll show." To empty, she may take an emetic (a substance that makes one vomit) like ipecac or stick her fingers (perhaps a toothbrush) down her throat far enough to gag and then vomit. Eventually she may be able just to bend over and throw up.

She may also (perhaps instead of vomiting) consume laxatives or diuretics to "clean out" or at least believe she is flushing. She may exercise with fervor and constancy, perhaps swimming and running 5 to 10 or more miles every day, satisfying not a quest for fitness but quelling a dread of gaining. Or, for the same reason, she may diet stringently or fast. Often, episodes of bulimia alternate with those of normal eating, but soon she returns to the bingeing–purging ritual.

And when she does, she risks becoming continually hoarse, weak, shaky, and headachy; wearing thin the enamel on her teeth; getting dental cavities; tearing and bleeding from her esophagus; dehydrating; and suffering hypokalemia (potassium depletion from excessive vomiting that causes cardiac arrhythmias and possibly death). And when she does, she hurtles her self-esteem to an all-time low, saddens, feels hopeless, and may try suicide.

Bulimia is a puzzle. Like the anorexic, the bulimic does it to herself. Or does she? The condition occurs not in isolation but in a climate of television ads and plots, movies, magazines, billboards, friends, relatives, and peers that cries out, "Be thin to be beautiful, to be accepted, to look good, to be good."

Attempts to solve the riddle of bulimia have tried to expose its ties with altered brain chemistry, insufficiency of the hunger-ending hormone cholecystokinin (CCK), family problems, overconcern with dieting by a parent, history of being sexually abused, and distorted thoughts. No one explanation fits all bulimics.

The bulimic may be certain that weight determines worth: "If I get overweight and fat, I'll be nothing, I'll fail." She may be positive she must be perfect, sure that if her clothes don't fit impeccably, if her hair doesn't lay exactly, if her skin doesn't glow flawlessly, she will be rejected by all who notice. And she is sure all will notice. "How I look is who I am; looks are everything, the everything everyone sees and cares about."

She may be convinced that if she does not weigh herself before and after each meal, before and after each run, before and after each bowel movement, she will gain. Preoccupied with weight, she may delude herself into thinking that frequent vomiting won't hurt her: "It'll keep me thin, nothing bad will happen."

Although she bows low to the goddess of thinness, she will spend much time thinking about the nemesis of this goddess: food. Sometimes, it becomes difficult to concentrate on anything but food. Yet, she may be certain that once full, she will be knocking at the fatness door. Her image of her body monopolizes her thoughts.

She may binge when she thinks about food or feels that she has been insulted or slighted. She may binge when she feels in violation of her dietary rules, slipped from the "right," from the perfect. She may binge when she feels that her body does not measure up to her rigid standards of beauty. She may so restrict her eating that she sets herself up to binge.

And because of her intense anxiety over getting fat, she will follow each binge with a purge. If she only binged, she would grow obese, as some young and older men and women find out. (Bingeing, by itself, is disordered eating.)

CC

When 17, Cleo-Cara (CC) came to me for treatment of her bulimia. Worried about the damage she was doing to her throat and mouth by repeated vomiting and aware that the bingeing–purging ritual was taking its toll on her self-esteem, CC's physician referred her for psychological help. An attractive teenager, CC appeared carefree and happy. Callouses on the backs of her index and middle fingers, however, betrayed the possibility of a sinister problem; the marks were from using her fingers to initiate vomiting. She told me of past anorexia and current bulimia:

When I was 14, I dieted to the point I stopped eating more than half a meal a day. I really got thin, too thin, so I gained. When I was a junior in high school, I learned I could eat everything, even ice cream and fudge, and still not get fat. I'd rather be a skeleton than blubbery, but I really love to eat. Jacki [a close friend] told me if I vomit right after I pig out, I'll stay thin.

I've been doing that for a year, eating and then vomiting, but lately haven't been feeling so good; besides, when I throw up, I'm disgusted with myself. Even brushing my teeth afterwards doesn't erase the sour taste in my mouth. I binge and vomit about three times a day.

Because I skip breakfast and lunch, I'm usually famished before I binge. But sometimes I'm not hungry in the slightest. Occasionally, I bake peanut-butter cookies; everyone in the family loves them. What no one knows is that for each dozen I make for my brother and parents, I make two dozen for me. I hide them until I need them.

I binge when no one is home. The smell of the cookies baking can get me going. So can seeing something advertised on daytime television. If what I see looks good, I'll go to the market and find it. I'll buy it, a cake, and a pound of maple fudge. Or, I'll buy a dozen doughnuts, two quarts of almond ice cream, and several candy bars. I'll lay everything on the kitchen counter and then, as fast as I can, stuff it.

When I finish everything or when Marty [her younger brother] comes home, I stop. Then, I head for the toilet, turn on the bath water to block out the vomiting sound, and get rid of what I've eaten. To make sure I get it all up, I sometimes start off with licorice or something else I can see in the vomit; I eat this marker stuff first, so it's last to come up; that way if I see it, I know I've cleared everything.

It has taken many sessions for CC to divulge she feels ugly and unintelligent—she is neither. During this time, she has revealed triggers of bingeing other than feeling hungry, smelling cookies baking, and seeing delectable foods advertised on television. When she sees a shapely girl in class or in the hall at school, she plans a later binge. When an attractive boy snubs her, she binges soon after the slight. When she feels down, whatever the reason, she arranges a binge.

Current treatment focuses on CC's thoughts about herself and about her reactions to her world. She has attempted methods to curb her binges and to handle the anxiety after bingeing that leads her to purge. She understands how she and society join forces to trouble her, and she feels better about who she is:

I don't want to be fat, and neither does anyone else, but if I eat normally I won't balloon up. Even if I gain, I'm more than bulges and curves.

Eating Disorder Alert

If you believe you have or are on the verge of having an eating disorder, consult your family physician. Also, watch for these signs:

- Never satisfied with your weight: Each low weight becomes the current high weight you dare not exceed—new lows immediately become new highs
- Have become very light, 15% or more below what is typical for your age, sex, and height
- Friends and family repeatedly say you are getting too thin
- Feel trapped by and preoccupied with food
- Afraid of gaining weight or fat and so check your weight frequently each day
- Feel fat despite others saying you are skinny
- Think continually about the shape of your body
- Usually down on how you look
- Endlessly exercising to control your weight
- Often fast to control your weight
- Often diet stringently to control your weight
- Binge once or more a week
- During a binge feel that food is your master
- Believe the only way to control your life is to starve or semistarve
- Self-induce vomiting, take laxatives, take diuretics
- For females, menstrual cycles irregular or cease

Control overweight without denying excessively. Eat better. Limit mildly. Expect lapses in overweight control to be temporary and mendable. Do not refuse yourself adequate nutrition or jeopardize yourself by playing thinning games that can ultimately fatten you, sicken you, sadden you, emaciate you, kill you.

EATING SENSIBLY

Acquiring good eating habits during the teenage years is wise because today's habits become tomorrow's. The kinds and portions of food you choose now will be those you will choose later, when an adult; though modifiable, habits built early resist change.

Acquiring good eating habits during the teen years is also wise because, Dr. Jean Mayer notes, these are the times for growing.[21] As nutrition experts Janet Christian and Dr. Janet Gregor of the University of Wisconsin explain, between the 10th and 14th year the typical girl shoots up under a foot and gains 40 to 50 pounds. Likewise, between his 12th and 16th year, the typical boy sprouts about a foot and puts on 50 to 60 pounds.[22] These are averages. Individuals grow at different rates, but differences aside, each person requires good nutrition to grow well.

And that means getting from food what is needed to live and prosper. About this, the Food and Nutrition Board of the National Research Council, today's authority on nutrition in the United States, says:

(Recommended Dietary Allowances) RDAs are . . . the levels of intake of essential nutrients that, on the basis of scientific knowledge, are judged . . . to be adequate to meet the known nutrient needs of practically all healthy persons. (p. 1)[23]

Appendix 1 lists these RDAs. It does not and could not consider each person's special needs that are related to illness, dieting, exercising. Talk to your physician or a dietitian about your unique situation.

To get what's recommended, say Christian and Gregor, choose foods daily from the different food groups, which give you carbohydrate, protein, fat, and water—the macronutrients—and vitamins and minerals—the micronutrients. Select from fruit and vegetables, meat and meat alternates (e.g., nuts, peas, beans, fish, chicken, turkey), milk and milk products (e.g., milk, cheese, yogurt), and grains (e.g., cereal, rice, tortillas, pasta). Vary choices day to day, selecting different members of the different groups on different days. What's more, limit (don't eliminate) sugars added to foods; sugar gives calories, that's about all.

As well, limit (don't eliminate) fats, advises *The Food Guide Pyramid,* a valuable booklet on nutrition put out by the United States Department of Agriculture.[24] The booklet cautions that some foods prepared one way are higher in fat than the same foods prepared another: A serving of french fries has twice the fat as a serving of scalloped potatoes. And some foods from the same food group are nearly fat-free, while others of the group are fat-loaded: A medium-size apple has only a trace of fat, whereas an avocado has nine grams of it.

According to the *Pyramid* and the bible on Recommended Dietary Allowances, don't take in more than 30% of the day's calories as fat.[25] And, they warn, reduce saturated fat (fat found in many cheeses, milk [except skimmed], butter, meats, and oils) to an upper limit of under 10%. If on a regimen of 1900 calories a day, 30% from fat means 570 calories from fat (1900×0.30):

$$\text{Fat Calories} = \text{Day's Total Calories} \times 0.30$$
$$[\text{Fat Calories} = 1900 \times 0.30 = 570 \text{ calories}]$$
$$\text{Grams of Fat} = \text{Fat Calories}/9$$
$$[\text{Grams of Fat} = 570/9 = \text{slightly over } 63 \text{ g}]$$

So, if on 1900 calories a day, trim fat to no more than 30%—try not to exceed 63 grams of fat per day, about 570 calories. Some nutrition authorities say thin the diet even further, to 25% fat.

Watch carefully. On their products, food packagers list how much fat a serving has. A package of easy-to-grab wheat snacks might print that 5 grams of one serving come from fat and that a serving has 100 calories—45 calories [5 × 9] or 45% of the serving are from fat. Five grams of fat may seem small, but 45% fat is not small.

I love granola. Each serving of my favorite brand has over 140 calories and more than 6 grams of fat; nearly 40% of the calories are from fat (54/140). But the packager's idea of a serving is a few bites: 30 grams. Because I can hold more than my parakeet does, I eat 90-gram servings. For me, grams of fat from this breakfast food, which now only infrequently do I have, are well over 18 g; 162 calories are from fat.

Eating less fat means eating more sensibly. Eating less fat helps you slim sensibly.

More about the Pyramid

In its 29 pages, the *Food Guide Pyramid* (obtained by writing to the Human Nutrition Information Service at the U.S. Department of Agriculture, 6505 Belcrest Road, Hyattsville, Maryland 20782) gives levelheaded eating tips. Five food groups, each recommending a range of servings per day, form it. At its bottom lies the bread, cereal, rice, and pasta group; 6 to 11 servings are advised. Immediately above this group are the vegetable—3 to 5 servings—and fruit groups—2 to 4 servings. Above them are the milk, yogurt, and cheese group—2 to 3 servings—and the meat, poultry, fish, dry beans, eggs, and nuts group—2 to 3 servings.

At the top of the pyramid are fats, oils, and sweets. To cut down fat, the pyramid advises:

- Remove skin from chicken and turkey
- Cut away fat on beef
- Choose lean cuts of beef, broiling or roasting instead of frying
- Drink low-fat or skim milk rather than whole milk
- Be conservative in how many nuts you eat
- Be conservative in how much fatty toppings, like mayonnaise and salad dressings, you dress up vegetables with
- Pick unsaturated vegetable oils and margarines
- Look carefully at product labels when deciding what to buy

The pyramid's theme . . . Eat well, stay well. Sample the five food groups each day. And, so readers are told, do not trade off servings in one group for servings in another or undercut serving ranges. If you breakfast on orange juice, a banana, two slices of margarine-laden toast (1 teaspoon of margarine), and 2% milk (1 cup), the pyramid says you have eaten five of your day's servings. And, if on a 2000-calorie diet, you have eaten 11 g of your day's upper limit of approximately 67 grams of fat. According to the pyramid, three-quarters of a cup of fruit juice without added sugar equals one serving from the fruit group, and so does the banana. Two pieces of toast with margarine equals two servings from the bread, cereal, rice, and pasta group and 6 grams of fat—close to 1 g for each slice of bread and about 4 g for the margarine. One cup of 2% milk amounts to one serving and 5 g of fat. Had you chosen skim milk, servings would not have changed but grams of fat from milk would have been just a trace.

Suppose instead of the toast and 2% milk, you decide to have whole milk and a medium danish with the same amount of margarine as before; you still include the juice and banana in the morning meal. The pyramid shows that your servings remain at five, but the amount of fat jumps to 25 g—2.3 times more than before. If hungry and you double the sweetrolls and margarine, servings go up by 2 and fat by 17 g. To control overweight, the toast breakfast outdoes the two others.

This chapter adds dieting to the basics touched on. As the next chapter begins to prove, overweight control requires more.

CHAPTER 4

TEENS IN CHARGE

PREPARING YOURSELF

Sitting and watching television one evening, you see a beautiful slender model appear on the screen. About 5 feet 8 inches and not an ounce over 120 pounds, she looks as if her pants have been spray-painted onto her skin and as if her sweater has been molded to her curves. Tight and revealing describe her outfit. As she vents the reasons you should buy the speedy, sleek car she drapes over, her underlying message shouts, "Those who are like me like those who like this car."

Comparing yourself to her, you feel bad. You are a young woman of 17, 5 feet 6 inches and 193 pounds. *If I dressed like her,* you say to yourself, *I'd bulge everywhere. I'm overweight. I'd better reduce, quickly.*

Or suppose you are a 16-year-old, 240-pound young man gazing enviously at a rented video of some shirtless hero attired in little more than a loincloth. Muscles rippling, this perfect specimen, this mighty V-shape, easily crushes his foes. The distance between this bronze 6 foot 3 inch warrior's shoulders exceeds by nearly 20 inches the circumference of his washboard waist.

That's how I want to look, you sigh inwardly. Well on your way to reaching his height, you are still an inverted V. *I'd better lose weight, fast.*

Better not, for quick loss is often temporary loss and can be unhealthy. Unless for some medical reason your physician wants you to take off pounds fast, do not try to reduce rapidly. Maybe after asking yourself the questions I pose next you will not want to try to reduce at all.

QUESTIONS TO ASK AND WAYS TO ANSWER

Before you try to trim down, ask and answer these questions.

Am I Heavy?

You think you are too heavy because of what peers, brothers, and sisters tell you. Sometimes they are cruel intentionally: You hear, "Hey, fat ass or fat f---," as you hang up your jacket in your locker, or "You're really a slob," as you suit up for volleyball. A nearby buffoon cannot resist publicly humiliating you. You are blamed for the scar.

Sometimes the comments are supposed to help, but they hurt; to me, these are the worst. Sincerely and solemnly, as if privy to some hidden truth, Murray, my close friend in high school, said, "You know, Mike, you'd really be nice-looking, if you'd lose 40 pounds." No sooner had his mouth erupted these words, I wanted to tape shut his lips. Why I wanted to, I didn't then know. Murray had crushed and insulted me.

Sometimes parents try to give you the "you're too fat" wisdom. "That white skirt would look even better on you, if you dropped 10 pounds." Or, a well-meaning yet insensitive teacher says, "You know, Margo, your face is really pretty," implying by what she does not say that the rest of you is not. No matter if the messages are cruel by design or by accident, you may begin to embrace them.

Another way you may come to believe you are heavy is through a morning ritual: awakening, standing naked atop the bathroom scale, reading the number in its tiny window. Panicking. But the anxiety may be needless, for the number may be false. Lean slightly to the left or right and perhaps you are heavier than if you were to stand straight on it. Step off the scale and wait 10 minutes; you may get a different reading, regardless of your position. Move the scale a few inches and readings may change, especially if the scale sits on a rug. Scales sometimes lie.

A third way you may learn to think of yourself as heavy happens at the doctor's. She or he weighs you on an accurate upright, springless, beam-balance scale and concludes you are too heavy. To diagnose you, the doctor probably consults special charts that show what others your age, sex, and height typically weigh. One of the most studied of these charts is the National Center for Health Statistics (NCHS) norms, which I have reproduced in Appendix 3.

Suppose you are a 14-year-old, 5 foot 5 inch girl. According to this chart, young women your age and height are at the 75th percentile in height, which means that only about 25% of the 14 and female set is taller than you are. On average, girls like you weigh about 125 pounds. You weigh nearly 140 pounds. Probably the doctor will not say you are too heavy. But he or she may watch how quickly you gain as you grow.

Suppose instead you weigh 170 pounds. Now, chances are, the doctor will label you overweight. Your weight is 36% above what is typical of others your age, height, and sex—20% higher is thought enough by many to call someone overweight. If also you have high blood pressure, high blood cholesterol, or other signs of actual or impending illness, likely you will be told to eat better and exercise more; such trouble signs often respond well to such improvements. You may also receive a target weight, a goal, a weight thought to be right for you. But what is right today may not be right tomorrow, because standards change as we learn more about what good health requires.

Useful as they are, explain researchers Drs. R. DuRant and C. Linder, the NCHS norms have such drawbacks as failing to say how heavy is too heavy or if where one lives (the North, South, East, or West) affects weight.[1]

And they do not say how much of what there is extra is fat, a topic to which we now turn.

Am I Fat?

Heaviness is not always fatness. Fatness is not always heaviness. Suppose you are 17, a boy in high school. Arriving at school each day by car, you sit at desks, walk from class to class, and visit the library. You often cut gym or finagle excuses from it because you hate exercise. At day's end, you ride home, watch television, do homework, and snack. You would rather ride everywhere than walk anywhere. For someone even to ask you to carry something imposes. You do not have the time to labor, so do not have an after-school job. No one suggests you are overweight— not parents, not doctors, not teachers, not friends.

Yet, you are as squeezable as a rubber toy and are sprouting love-handles. Weight-scale readings do not shock you, weight-chart numbers do not upset you. But you are fat.

Unlike the sedentary boy, you are the same age, you love football, baseball, basketball, and running and undeniably are a V-shape. The scale weighs you heavy because the weight of your muscles pushes the needle far above the typical weight of others your age, sex, and height. Yet, in no way are you fat: shoulders broad, arms and legs sinuous, waist small and firm.

For neither boy will weight scales separate fat from all else that is not fat. Scales tell only about weight, not about what the weight comprises, not about how many of the pounds are of fat. Heaviness or bigness does not definitely mean fatness.

What others say influences whether you see yourself as fat. Again, peers, friends, and relatives often find it difficult to remain silent on the subject of your shape and may freely advise that you are too fleshy. They may say you eat too much, or move too little, or both overeat and underexercise. They may intend or not intend to be nasty, but they are nasty. Soon, you may agree with the cruelest of your detractors—almost as if the worst is easiest to believe.

Judging if you are too fat is also influenced by the mirror test. Stripped, you stand before the mirror and see short legs and a larger-than-you-would-like-to-have derriere. But concluding you are too fat may misinterpret the changes in your body that adolescence brings. Like the mirror test, the clothes test (new tightness in formerly well-fitting garments) may cause you to view natural gains in size as unwanted gains in fat. Speaking about muddling big with fat, nutrition researchers Drs. Jean Mayer and Johanna Dwyer of Tufts note that many obese girls hate what they cannot change:

. . . few obese adolescents seem to be aware of the fact that many of the characteristics they dislike about their bodies (e.g., width of chest, length of legs, position of waist, etc.) are more directly related to build than to fatness. (p. 105)[2]

Ask your family doctor whether you are too fat. She may send you to someone who will (or will herself) measure fat at specific places on your body by sizing circumferences or by calipering skinfolds, or by doing both the sizing and the calipering. Calipering entails pinching up folds of skin and measuring their thicknesses. Those assessing skinfold thicknesses use an instrument having arms that close down on the skin and that exert constant pressure at the pinching site: the triceps (back of the arm midway between the shoulder and elbow), the subscapular (back of the shoulder), or other sites. At our clinic, we employ an 11-inch-long scissors-like device (Harpenden calipers). To evaluate degree of slimming, we monitor skinfold thickness changes during treatment. Pinching is painless.

Will My Problems Disappear If I Trim Down?

Since the age of 10, Brad has believed he was fat. Now 16, he weighs 205 pounds and stands 5 feet 9 inches. His shoulders are too narrow and his waist, thighs, and buttocks too large, so he thinks. Shy and friendless, he does occasionally spend time with Rob, but Rob has many other friends he prefers, and Brad knows it.

Although Brad expects it and although he hates it, he is teased at school about his body. Sometimes, he laments to himself, *They must think "fat ass" is my nickname.* Never does he ask a question in class for fear of drawing attention to himself; he waits until everyone but the teacher leaves. Never does he talk to Lisa Deane, the attractive new girl in Geography, though she fills his daydreams. He thinks, *If only I could be like muscular Joe Carson, whose waist is like a pencil, I'd talk to Lisa, even date her.*

Perhaps because he feels bad about his body, rejected and rejectable, Brad is shy. Trimming down may help him feel better about himself, but it will not automatically and immediately make him outgoing and confident. Likely, if he feels better about himself, he will, psychologists agree, capitalize on some opportunities to acquire social skills. Yet losing weight will not by itself make him socially facile. It may start the process, that's all.

Do I Want to Trim Down?

This question asks about commitment, about willingness to try to control overweight. If you cannot commit to the discipline and the boredom of daily efforts to reduce overweight, freely commit to eating differently and to exercising more, do not begin. Do not be bullied, forced, or embarrassed into going on an overweight control program. Hold off until ready, which may be next week, next month, next year, or never.

To decide when you are ready, do something like Drs. Daniel Kirschenbaum, William Johnson, and the late Peter Stalonas write about in *Treating Childhood and Adolescent Obesity:* Fold a piece of paper lengthwise; title one column "pro" and the other "con"; list why to commit to a program under "pro" and why not to under "con." Table 4.1 illustrates ten reasons under "pro" ("I'll look much better on the beach in summer") and five under

TABLE 4.1. Deciding about a Program

What I want to happen: *Lose 25 pounds*

By when do I want it to happen:

Date begin: November 1
Date end: October 31   12 months

Pro reasons

—The teasing about my weight will end.
—More people will want me around.
—Clothes will fit better.
—I'll get invited to more parties.
—I'll be staying home fewer Saturday nights.
—I'll go to more dances.
—I'll look much better on the beach in summer.
—I'll have better selections of clothes.
—I'll be focusing on me for me.
—My parents will stop nagging me about my weight.

Con reasons

—People at school will tease me for dieting.
—I'll be caving in to the thin-crazy world.
—If I go out more, my grades will drop.
—Losing 25 pounds is too hard.
—People will recall my heavy days and broadcast it in front of me, and that's embarrassing.

"con" ("People will recall my heavy days and broadcast it in front of me and that's embarrassing").

Tally entries; compare columns. In the table, there are twice as many "pro" items as "con" items—good reason to decide for overweight control. But consider well each point on the list, for doing so may clarify the decision, as the authors explain. Perhaps, the "con" of "losing 25 pounds is too hard" is so negative it matters more than do two or three of the reasons on the "pro" list. Possibly easing the goal of 25 pounds to 20 pounds and giving yourself more time to attain it, 15 months instead of 12, will make the weight hurdle less formidable. Revise goals to make negatives less negative, positives more positive. You have to want to trim. Dr. Kirschenbaum and colleagues write:

> . . . the person who cannot make a very clear commitment to lose weight is virtually guaranteed to fail at any such attempt. (p. 20)[3]

What Should My Goals Be?

Say you opt for a program. You want to lose weight and because, to you, life is hell, you want to lose it fast. So, you set yourself a goal of dropping 50 pounds in 10 weeks. You starve. A week of this self inflicted, ill-conceived torture is all you can stand. Your unhealthy program is doomed to fail, because losing 5 pounds a week for 10 weeks is close to impossible without winding up in the hospital.

Now knowing this, you decide not to fast, not to harm yourself, not to embark on a search for improbable, hurtful, unsustainable change. Instead, after consulting with your family's doctor, you pick a reasonable goal reflecting current amount overweight. Using the NCHS norms and a formula employed by the Baylor researchers Foreyt and Goodrick,[4] the doctor says you are nearly 32% overweight. Few of your peers, those your age, sex, and height, weigh as much.

The doctor arrives at 32% by determining what your peers typically weigh—a possible goal weight for you—and dividing your current weight by that possible goal weight; to get a percent, he multiplies the result by 100.

$$\text{Overweight \%} = \frac{\text{starting weight}}{\text{goal weight}} \times 100$$

If 13 years old, female, and 5 feet 3 inches tall, you are near the 75th percentile in height on the NCHS norms; only about 25% of other girls your age are taller than you. A good weight, the typical weight of 5 foot 3 inch, 13-year-old girls at the 75th percentile, is about 114 pounds.

Think of it this way. To be as heavy as you are tall, you should be at the 75th percentiles in weight and height. Weighing 150 pounds makes you 36 pounds heavier than girls as old and as tall as you. Weighing 150 pounds is weighing in the range of a 13-year-old at about the 95th percentile, a weight of someone typically over 5 feet 6 inches. Divide today's actual weight by today's goal weight to get percent overweight:

$$\text{Overweight \%} = \frac{150 \text{ pounds}}{114 \text{ pounds}} \times 100$$
$$= 132\% \ (32\% \text{ overweight})$$

Note, there is good news. Over the many months it will take to lose the extra 36 pounds, you will grow in height; doing so reduces the amount you are overweight even if weight were to stay the same. The taller you are, the heavier you can be and not be overweight. As well, percent overweight depends on age. You need not lose as much as you think.

Possibly, from the start, you will not be asked to shed some total number of pounds. Instead, the objective might be small weekly reductions—perhaps one-fourth pound every seven days or so. Losing weekly aligns the height and weight percentiles on NCHS norms. So do the next two goals. Instead of emphasizing total or weekly loss, however, they focus on reducing rate, speed, of gaining. If you are adding pound after pound week after week, slowing gaining helps, as does, for a time, stopping gaining altogether; diminishing or eliminating gaining while still growing are good aims for overweight teenagers.

Goals could be unrelated to losing weight. After talking it over with his physician, one young man I know decided he wanted to wear pants that did not billow like sails. Tracking progress by trying on new pants each week, he thrilled over inches lost from his 38 inch middle. When comfortable in size 30 pants, he stopped his program.

One can combine losing weight with subtracting inches from the waist, hips, and thighs. Or, one can join the hope of fitting better in clothes with goals of increasing stamina, decreasing stress to joints, reducing blood pressure, reducing cholesterol, or being healthier (see Chapter 10). A program may have several purposes. Table 4.2 summarizes possible program goals.

Who Helps?

Look to brothers, sisters, friends, uncles, aunts, doctors, psychologists, psychiatrists, school psychologists, teachers,

TABLE 4.2. Possible Program Goals[a]

Weight-related goals

Aligning the height and weight percentiles

- Losing a specified number of pounds (even just a few pounds) over a lengthy period
- Losing small amounts weekly (not every week will there be a loss)
- Diminishing the rate of gaining while growing in height (especially for mildly to moderately overweight and younger teenagers)
- Eliminating gaining while growing in height

Fat-related goals

- Reducing selected circumferences (e.g., waist) to change the wardrobe
- Having clothes you currently own fit better

Health-related goals

- Lessening the waist/hips ratio
- Lowering blood pressure
- Lowering blood cholesterol
- Lessening diabetes risk factors
- Lessening exertion difficulties
- Lessening stress to weight-bearing joints

[a] There may be two or more of some of these goals at the same time.

therapists, dietitians, grandparents, and parents for help. Ask for their assistance. Ask them to help you choose and reach manageable, meaningful ends. Do not bear the burden of an overweight control program alone.

Encourage success; seek support. Your doctor may help you set goals. Your parents may promise you money for living up to goals. Your school psychologist may recommend procedures; your grandparents may swear to stop pushing candy and other treats; your brothers and sisters may promise to stop teasing. Near the end of the program, your parents may agree to give you greater rewards for your continuing to live up to goals, because following the program gets harder, later. Support, maintain psychologists Lisa Buckmaster of Willamette University and Kelly Brownell of Yale, means others in your world help you—emotionally, educationally, financially.[5]

Support does not mean control. Supporters do not force; they guide. Hunt for control of yourself by yourself, not by others. Sometimes, as the next example shows, parents govern too much, and this may cause problems.

The Case of Craig Watters

Blonde Craig Watters was 15 years old and heavy. Although his Levis fit loosely and his dark long-sleeved shirt hung untucked, he believed he could not hide the fatness of his 200-pound, 5 foot 10 inch body; to Craig, his waist was huge and his body flabby. According to the NCHS norms, Craig exceeded the 95th percentile in weight and was just below the 90th percentile in height; goal weight was roughly 158 pounds—the weight of 15-year-old boys slightly under the 90th percentile in height. He was, therefore, about 42 pounds overweight.

Pounds overweight = present weight − goal weight
200 pounds − 158 pounds
= 42 pounds overweight

As for percent overweight, Craig was close to 127% of what others his age, sex, and height weigh (200 pounds/ 158 pounds $\times$ 100), or 27% overweight.

Craig's parents, two younger twin sisters (Janice and Janet), and older college-age brother (Bob) were thin. Craig hated being the only overweight member of his prosperous, educated, middle-class family. "I must have bad genes," he would say to his mother and father, trying to evoke guilt but causing anger instead. In defense, they would answer with tone and words to shame him, "You eat way too much, Craig, and that's why you're so heavy."

Eager to lose weight, he talked to his parents and family doctor. He wanted to drop 60 pounds in four months. His parents wanted him to do that, too, but his physician opted for less loss over more time and asked Craig to call me for methods.

When I first met Craig, I was struck by his intelligence, knowledge, and assertiveness. He played the clarinet skill-fully, collected old comics, coins, and stamps avidly, and attacked puzzles (math and word) brilliantly. Although the butt of "fat jokes" in school and at home, he was outgoing and felt good about himself. He considered his detractors, brother and sisters included, jerks. After he read several books I gave him on overweight control, we devised a program we thought rational and workable. It failed . . . at first.

Craig was to observe what, how often, and how much he ate and how much he exercised at school. I gave him forms to make records (Chapter 5). Also, he was to ask his parents to finance the weight-loss deals he made with himself, to join both parents in their jointly taken after-dinner walks, and to plan menus with his mother—the cook in this robust family of six. What's more, by such requests as asking that food be kept only in the kitchen, he was to try to improve the eating layout of his home. His goal: lose a few pounds while growing.

He did ask his parents for help, but they in their zeal to see him thin volunteered more than help. Mom said she would cook nutritious, low-calorie fare for the whole family. Both mother and father told Craig not to worry about recording what he ate and how much he exercised at school. They would record. "Concentrate on schoolwork and leave the other stuff to us. Just tell us about snacks at home and elsewhere, and sports at school." As for financing the program, his parents refused. Giving money for reducing was, to them, bribery (Chapter 6) and not only unnecessary but also unwholesome. Whatever needed change, they would tell Craig about, and he would comply because, as they said: "After all, losing weight is your idea, Craig."

For two weeks, Craig prospered—lost two pounds. But by the end of week three, he started to regain, and by the end of week four, not a speck taller, he was heavier than when he had begun.

Unhappy, Craig told me that the program belonged to his parents, not to him: "It's like I'm in the fourth grade again. They're hovering over me. I hate that. They've made Bob, Janice, and Janet "Eat Smart," that's what they call the kind of meals we now get, and those guys blame me for the lean times. Bob and the girls are meaner than ever."

I asked, "Do you dislike the program because of the results or is it that you hate how it's being run?"

"Both, I don't know, but I don't want to try anymore. I'd rather go back to the old way, the way things used to be at home."

"Why don't you talk to your parents and ask them to let you record and help plan menus. Maybe if you help plan them, there will be more of what everyone wants; you can bring in nutritious, lower-calorie, lower-fat foods gradually. Ask them to help you out with money to run the program. Tell them the money's not a bribe but a way for you to live up to the program, for you to get over the rough spots."

After talking again with his parents, Craig got them to agree, albeit reluctantly, to his requests, saying that they would reevaluate everything in a month. Though still feeling watched, he retrieved control and marshaled support. And motivation returned. After one year and five changes in his program, he had lost and grown enough to be no longer overweight.

Because he got older and taller, his *goal weight, zero percent overweight,* changed from that of a younger, shorter boy to that of an older, taller boy. Craig's real goal was not to get to 158 pounds but to get to zero percent overweight. That he did, indeed. As he aged and grew, the weight that meant zero percent overweight increased from 158 pounds, making the goal more and more attainable.

From this case history, I cannot say that Craig's conviction that his parents ran the program ruined the program. But from observing teenagers I treat, I believe they do better when they are in charge. Research supports my contention. Dr. Esther Cohen of the University of the Pacific and her associates suggest that when parents take over overweight-control jobs, such as tracking their son's or daughter's daily foods, the successful young people do not stay successful.[6] After treatment ends, they do not do as well as the stay-in-charge teenagers.

Of the 10- to 17-year-olds the Cohen group studied, 25 had received treatment for being overweight. The question was: Do these young people, average age about $13\frac{1}{2}$, keep thinner and, if so, what influences how well they do? The experimenters learned that those who did more on their own behalf after treatment fared better than did those who let their parents take over after it. But, as the authors inquire, do parents control more when sons and daughters begin to slide, or do sons and daughters begin to slide when parents control more?

Ask for support, do not demand it, for the demand puts off others. Demanding that everyone in the family diet may cause your thinner brothers and sisters to rebel. Cajoling parents to support your contracts and finance your efforts may get you less than will requesting their help and explaining what you need.

Table 4.3 lists potential supporters and how they might help. Not everyone listed can do every job listed, and sometimes the table has two or more persons doing the same job. Gauge who can do what for you. Talk to potential helpers about what you hope they can and will do.

There's No One to Help

Are you sure? Even if both parents work outside the home and are away from it much of the time, they can assist you: stock snacks like fruits and vegetables; plan with you the breakfasts, lunches, and dinners; finance the program. Explore the possibilities the table offers. When there is no one besides a physician to help, you still have options. You still may control your foods, exercises, behaviors.

TABLE 4.3. Potential Helpers and How They Might Help[a]

Helper	Possible help given
Doctor	• Checks your health
	• Checks health risks
	• Measures percent overweight
	• Takes fatness measurements
	• Advises on calorie needs
	• Advises on nutritional needs
	• Advises on exercise needs
	• Names other helpers to talk to
School psychologist	• Helps design a program
Parents	• Help design a program
	• Help finance a program
	• Stock foods for dieting
	• Lessen stockpile of high-calorie, high-fat foods
	• Find nutritional bargains
	• Help create menus
	• Help create opportunities for exercise
Brothers and sisters	• Support your effort to control weight by not ridiculing it
Grandparents and other relatives	• Stop proffering rich treats
Teachers (e.g., physical education)	• Design conditioning regimens
	• Create opportunities for exercise

[a] Undoubtedly there are more potential helpers than I list, and the helpers I do list may do more jobs than I name.

What Should I Expect to Do?

When building a program from the principles and tactics this book names, you will do some of what follows:

- Observe and record how much, what, where, and when you eat and exercise. Find out about how your world affects your eating: about day-to-day routines, such as removing the garbage from the home and walking to school; about periodic recreations, such as playing volleyball, basketball, football; about planned exercises, such as jogging or swimming laps.
- Exercise more.
- Cut down on television.
- Eat better. Limit treats like potato chips, french fries, Pop Tarts, eclairs.
- Lower fat intake.
- Substitute fruits and vegetables for some rich snacks.
- Snack less when watching television.
- Remove obstacles blocking change: the presence of food, the sight of others eating, the kindness of a food-friend, the shame of being seen exercising, the discomfort of being tired or bored by exercise (Chapter 8).
- Monitor progress in modifying weight, sizes, fit of clothes, feelings, comments of others, self-statements.
- Control without medicating.
- Plan behaviors that gradually and progressively control overweight.

- Check with your physician for help when setting goals and calorie levels, upgrading nutrition, assessing growth, tabulating overweight and overfat.
- Enlist the support of others, including parents.
- Reward or remove rewards, perhaps through signed agreements.
- Plan and problem-solve to stand up for your rights, to think better of yourself, to rearrange your world—to remove disabling and to add enabling conditions.

Do not begin any program believing the following: If it fails, you fail; this is your last chance to reduce healthfully; being thin is undeniably and unimpeachably right; a thin body houses a strong character, an overweight body a weak one spellbound by demons of gluttony and sloth.

Are You Better Off for Having Been on a Program?

Do not begin any program believing that by becoming thin you abolish your woes, for, as discussed, successful overweight control does not automatically end problems. But it may bring these benefits:

Better Health

The doctor is the best person to answer health questions. If you began a program having high cholesterol, high blood pressure, exertion difficulties, and so on, find out if these health markers have corrected now that you have ended the program. Being the person to track your changing health picture, the doctor must be in on your program from its start.

Less Overweight

If your parents reduce, they score success by counting lost pounds. Provided that they did not fast, purge, or do something else unhealthy to drop weight, they would be correct. But if you measure progress by the pound, you could misconstrue no loss as failure, for you are still growing. Craig Watters failed to reach first goal weight, the weight set down when the program began, yet still lost enough to be no longer overweight by its end. To do this, he stayed on his program while growing taller, thereby changing his percent overweight.

You begin a program at 170 pounds and after nearly a year are lighter by 22 pounds. Quite a feat. But, suppose you lose nothing; the program has not necessarily failed. To see progress, calculate overweight change:

$$\text{Overweight change} = \frac{\text{beginning weight}}{\text{goal weight}} - \frac{\text{ending weight}}{\text{goal weight}}$$

If goal weight at the start, the typical weight of others your sex, age, and height, is 125 pounds and at the end of the program is 135 pounds, the program has done well:

$$\text{Overweight change} = \frac{170}{125} - \frac{170}{135} \text{ or}$$
$$1.36 - 1.26 = 0.10 \times 100 = 10\%$$

Stopping overweight from increasing is an achievement, losing 10% of it a triumph.

Clothes Fit Better

Clad in jeans, you appraise the mirror's reflection and feel happy, sad, or angry depending on the look. Although 50-year-olds, 30-year-olds, 20-year-olds, and teens differ from each other on what looks good, you know the unique standards of your particular group and whether you meet them. For some of you, it was the bad fit of clothes that started you thinking about overweight control. When after struggling to change shape, you find that clothes fit better, you rejoice. But this benefit is hard to quantify. Physicians, psychologists, nutritionists, and dietitians want to know not only what parts have changed but also by how much.

Sizes Change

Measure the circumferences of your arms, chest, waist, and thighs. Physical education teachers and physicians may also want to determine changes in one or more skinfolds.

More Stamina and Strength

Having undergone the exercise part of overweight control and having reduced percent overweight, you may now be more physically fit: You can swim farther and faster, do more sit-ups, do more pull-ups, run farther, jump higher. I remember that after months of walking, weight-lifting, and biking to reduce in my 17th year, my pull-ups increased 100%—from zero to one; a happy day for me, to be sure.

Many North American young people are physically unfit, write University of Massachusetts researchers Drs. Patty Freedson, James Rippe, and Ann Ward in *Turning*

Kids on to Fitness,[7] particularly, perhaps, those who are overweight.

Better Eating

Fear of being malnourished probably did not spur you on to control overweight, but you can be overweight and malnourished; not only the starving are undersupplied. Malnutrition, say nutrition writers Janet Christian and Janet Gregor, means "poor nutritional status resulting from intakes either above or below the beneficial range" (p. 9).[8]

By regulating consumption, you may have bettered nutrition: You may have cut down on cakes and ice cream; increased apples, pears, oranges, carrots, celery, and lettuce; reduced candy; reduced fast-foods; switched to skim milk; stopped coming home from school so famished that you snack voraciously and unwisely. To find out if you now get more of what Appendix 1 recommends, ask a physician or a dietitian.

Better Feelings about Yourself

Perhaps you put yourself through the rigors of overweight control because you despaired about being overweight and felt out of control. Perhaps now you feel better about yourself.

Better Behaviors

To change body shape, modify behavior. In this book, we assume that by lessening rich-food intake at home, by watching what you eat at the coffeeshop, by walking to and from school, by playing soccer or hockey during and after school, by limiting television to half your customary four hours each day, you will consume fewer calories from fat and burn more calories from exercise. And, if for weeks and weeks you endure such changes, the fit of your clothes will improve and the percent of your overweight will decline.

Mainly, this chapter has talked about readying for overweight control. The next one addresses a major part of actually doing it, observing and recording. Each of you must watch yourself and log what you see to know what you do, fail to do, need to do.

TEENS IN CHARGE ━━━━━━━━

WATCH YOURSELF AND MAKE RECORDS

This chapter asks you to observe yourself and take note of what you see.

WHY OBSERVE AND RECORD?

It is hard to remember two days ago—the foods for breakfast and dinner, the hours of television, the snacks while watching. It is nearly impossible to remember a week ago—whether you felt smart, good-looking, ugly, dumb, afraid, in control, out of control. To remember, you need records. However you note foods, exercises, behaviors, and feelings, do note them. By doing so, you begin to know yourself in a way that allows change.

Each afternoon you take the bus home from junior high; the bus stop is 15 steps from the school entrance. The bus comes and, in three minutes, you are a quarter mile down the road and in five at your front door. Moments after entering, you plop down on the living room couch and, just before your head hits cushion, grab and press the TV remote. On turns the television, off turns you. There, three hours immobile, entranced by daytime soaps and quiz shows, you lie until the snacking urge strikes or dinner is announced—sometimes fewer than 20 minutes separates craving and call.

Instead of describing your actions, you could label them, but that would be unproductive. If you use "lazy," all you have done is name-call. The nasty label only seems to explain why you do what you do. Worse, the label is useless and demeaning. It says you are weak or flawed and slaps at your dignity. Similarly, suppose one Saturday afternoon after coming home from the mall famished, you raid the cookie jar and down 15 cookies. Afterwards, angry at yourself, you say, "I'm a glutton." Words of self-contempt, more hateful than those from others, keep you away for a time from cookie jars, candy dishes, pies, cakes, ice cream. The unkind self-evaluation prompts change in eating habits, but the change will be short-lived and the change method is humiliating.

Using Figure 5.1, try monitoring, not name-calling, and record a day's eating. Note in the asterisked column if the meal is a snack [S], breakfast [B], lunch [L], or dinner [D]. Write down when you eat, what you eat, how much you eat, how you feel right before you eat (hungry, happy, angry, bored, sad, anxious), how many calories you consume, and what you do before, during, and after you eat. Once you have this information, a week or two of it is instructive; you will know how often you snack and on what you snack. You will know when and how often you eat. You will know if typically you accompany the pleasures of television and reading with those of eating. You will know the inside triggers, perhaps boredom and sadness, of your eating. You will know much about yourself, putting you in the commanding position to change yourself.

Date _____

Record after eating (* = meal or snack, Qn = quantity, cals = calories):

What doing?

Time   Mood   *   Food   Qn   Cals   Before   During   After

FIGURE 5.1. Form to record a day's eating.

WHAT TO WATCH AND HOW TO RECORD

You have choices. You could track walking, time watching television, snacking, out-of-home dining, thoughts, feelings, and more. Parents, physicians, psychologists, social workers, teachers, dietitians, or nutritionists can help you select targets.

Eating

We have just looked at Figure 5.1 for recording foods already eaten. You could instead record foods about to be eaten or, predicting longer, foods to be eaten in 6 to 24 hours; I like the long-range planning; one drawback is that its recording forms are complex (see Chapter 8).

A simple system is tracking food exchanges. In 1986, the American Diabetes Association and the American Dietetic Association published six food lists to plan meals with.[1] Originally for diabetics, the system helps nondiabetics, too. The six lists comprise starch/bread, milk, fruit, vegetables, meat/meat substitutes, and fat. The food exchanges, the foods in each category, are alike in calories and macronutrients. For example, selections in the starch/bread category are each close to 15 grams of carbohydrate, 3 grams of protein, and 80 calories.

Another easy system, this one offered by social worker Dr. Richard Stuart and nutrition practitioner-researcher Barbara Davis in their classic *Slim Chance in a Fat World*,[2] is designed for adults but is applicable (with more servings of milk) to teens. The Stuart and Davis approach tracks meat, cereal, milk, vegetables, fruit, and miscellaneous (fats, candy, syrup, sugar, soft drinks).

David Perry

Figure 5.2 shows the Stuart and Davis system in action. We used it to help David Perry, a 5 foot 11 inch, 15-year-old, 199-pound boy. According to David's doctor, who referred him, David could weigh at his height and age about 165 pounds; at treatment's start, David was close to being 21% overweight (199/165 × 100). On a diet of 1900 calories a day, David enjoyed a variety of exchanges.

Across the top of his exchange card, David wrote his daily allotment. Regularly filling it out, David would tabulate seven day's worth of diet data by the week's end. On the back of the card, he tracked his exercising and each failure (when and why) to live up to mapped-out exchanges.

Card entries told him and us how well he followed his program. Because he hated carrying the card to school, to restaurants, to movies, wherever he went, he carried cut-up, pocket-size pieces of paper instead. On them, he recorded the information for later transfer to his card, which for privacy he hid under his desk blotter at home. He sought help from not only his doctor and us but also his parents; they bankrolled his motivation by paying him when he progressed.

With his mother's help, David chose foods from the Stuart and Davis lists and planned his menus, allowing himself 300 calories a day of unplanned-for food—his slush fund for the unexpected foods he would surely have (Chapter 8). He expected the unexpected. He knew that visiting with a friend at the friend's home or walking to the convenience store near his school often led to unplanned-for snacking. Sometimes hours after laying out a food plan, David substituted one food for another.

	Meat	Cereal	Milk	Veg. & fruit	Misc.
Exchanges I'm allowed	7	8	3	7	7
Monday	XXXXX	XXXXXX	XXX	XXXXXXX	XXXX
Tuesday					
Wednesday					
Thursday					
Friday					
Saturday					
Sunday					

FIGURE 5.2. Exchange diet card. The exchanges allotted are from, in modified form, the 1900-calorie exchange diet of R. B. Stuart and B. A. Davis (1978). *Slim Chance in a Fat World. Condensed Edition Revised.* Champaign: Research Press. Misc. = fats, candy, syrup, sugar, soft drinks.

Substituting was okay provided that David not jump between food groups. If to meet one of his seven-a-day fruit and vegetable exchanges, he reluctantly agreed to celery but later did not want it, he could substitute tomato or lettuce or mushrooms, and so on; but he had to stay within the fruit and vegetable list. He couldn't trade celery for sausage—vegetable for meat.

In six months, David fell to about 10% overweight, where he now remains.

The Stop and Go Diet

To help overweight children, Dr. Leonard Epstein of the University of Buffalo and colleagues created the "stop-light" or "traffic light diet."[3] In a book about this way of watching foods, he and Sally Squires say overweight teenagers, as well as children, can use the system.[4]

The traffic light diet groups foods by calorie ranges— low, moderate, and high—and tracks the amount of nutrition each food yields. Foods labeled green (e.g., bouillon, club soda, mushrooms, lettuce, spinach) have few calories and many nutrients. Green foods, you need; eat plenty of them. Richer in calories, yellow foods (like green foods) are low fat and high nutrition. As the traffic light diet inventors maintain, you need yellows, too, but watch how many you eat.

For the most part, avoid foods labeled red: alcohol, high-fat foods, combinations over 350 calories a serving. In general, red foods are bad bargains—poor in nutrition, loaded with calories.

In traffic light terms, go with the green, slow (be cautious) with the yellow, and stop with the red. The green–yellow–red distinction crosscuts different food groups: There are yellows (cantaloupes, apricots, cherries) and reds (avocado, dried figs, raisins) in the fruit group; there are greens and reds (baked beans, hash browns, creamed vegetables) in the vegetable one. Easy to use, the stoplight diet improves nutrition and reduces overweight; it is well-suited to teenagers.

Activity

Strive for the active life. Burn enough calories regularly and you will slim, get fit, lose fat, be able to eat more without fattening, and possibly better hold up metabolic rate (Chapter 2).

One easy way to record activity is to write down hourly what you do. Similarly, a way Dr. Kirschenbaum and colleagues suggest, chart the entire day's exercises and their durations.[5] Still another way, fold a sheet of paper in half lengthwise. Down the left, the promise part, list the activities you want to do that day. Down the right, the performance part, list those you did do that day and for how long. Then, as Drs. Aaron Beck and David Burns of the University of Pennsylvania ask of their depressed patients, rate how pleasurable each activity was. Goals: Do more longer, like exercise better. Figure 5.3 pictures the form to use.

More complex, record daily routines, such as cleaning your bedroom, and recreations, such as swimming, after planning a week of them. Begin each week proposing new ways to be active. With this activity-adding system, you build onto the activity life.

Day & date:

Activities I hope to do   Activities I did P[a]

_____   _____

_____   _____

_____   _____

_____   _____

_____   _____

_____   _____

_____   _____

_____   _____

_____   _____

_____   _____

_____   _____

[a] Pleasure ranking: 1 = Unpleasant; 2 = Somewhat unpleasant; 3 = Neither pleasant nor unpleasant; 4 = Somewhat pleasant; 5 = pleasant.

FIGURE 5.3. Record of activities. Form proposed by Sharon Cairns.

Inactivity

Keeping records is about as much fun as licking stamps. You may hate recording so much so that you will fast to avoid it: no eating, no recording.

Better, you may reduce eating to reduce recording: forego the before-bed snack to escape the exchange card or data sheet. But avoiding exercise to avoid recording harms, as does fasting, for the goal is strengthening, not weakening, the activity life.

There is a way to dodge the recording chore while not dodging activity. Instead of recording action, record inaction. Figure 5.4 tracks doing nothing. On the form, blacken each 15-minute interval during which there is 10 minutes of inactivity (e.g., lying down, watching television, studying, listening to your teacher, listening to your parents, talking on the phone). The figure shows four days, day and night clocks. Each day has ninety-six 15-minute periods, 48 on the A.M. half and 48 on the P.M. half.

Some inactivity, like sleeping, lasts hours and cannot be recorded interval by interval. It would be absurd if I asked you to awaken every 15 minutes to keep data. Make records of sleeping and the like only when it is over: So, for sleeping, log the night's hours on arising—blacken the 28 spaces between midnight and 7 A.M. Blacken 4 spaces to cover the dinner hour, 8 spaces to handle two hours studying, 4 to record the hour on the phone, and 20 to chronicle the sedentary five hours of your six hours of school.

Television. Blacken 24 spaces on the activity clock if you have watched television from 4 P.M. to 6 P.M. and then again from 7 P.M. to 11 P.M.

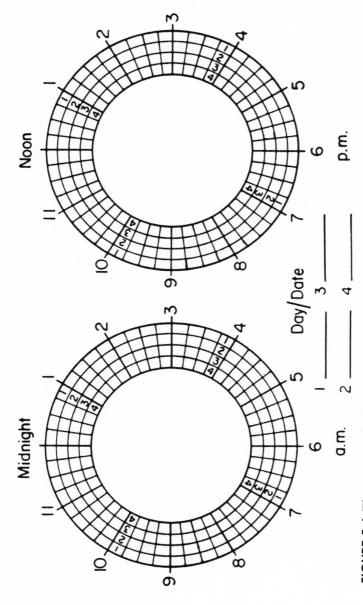

FIGURE 5.4. The activity clock. From H. A. Jordan, L. S. Levitz, and G. S. Kimbrell. Reprinted by permission.

Television watching is the quintessential modern inactivity. Doubtless, today's favorite pastime is gazing at the tube that transmits a world of fantasy into your living room. Television mesmerizes. In fact, Dr. William Dietz of Tufts University writes about a teenager whose metabolic rate was slower when the boy watched TV than when he did nothing.[6] That supports what many of us know firsthand: TV slows us down, almost hypnotizes us. We stare dreamlike as the story unfolds and let ourselves escape.

And escaping, some of us long for. When I was about 12 years old, fat, and the butt of fat jokes, television helped me cope with the venomous, antifat world. It soothed me and, so I thought at the time, protected me. But possibly it harmed me, for it allowed me to run away instead of face my peers. As well, because it became my main waking inactivity, it made me fatter and less physically fit. Dr. Larry Tucker of Brigham Young University investigated whether watching television each day affected the physical condition—ability to do pull-ups, sit-ups, sidestep, run, push-ups. Testing 379 teenage boys, he indeed found a relationship—heavy watching (more than four hours a day), lower fitness.[7]

TV lulls you into nothingness as it gives to you, gets to you, and takes from you. Because the TV made me fatter, it escalated the rejection I felt and, to escape, the isolation I sought. The more I watched, the more overweight I became. This watching-fattening, warns Dr. Dietz, may happen to many young people.[8]

Also, he cautions, TV goads you into rich eating. Commercials are less likely to promote carrots, lettuce, tomatoes, oranges, and pears than to hawk chips, dip, sugary cereal, Pop Tarts, and candy. High-calorie consumption grosses billions of dollars yearly.

There is something else that TV does. Its stars are usually lean, and the message viewers get is that these chosen ones, these gods and goddesses, will stay lean no matter what they eat. Says the TV by endorsing rich high-fat food, "Eat what you will, you will not fatten." As Dr. Dietz points out, this is the contradiction the bulimic lives—eat everything, stay thin.[9]

Record how long you spend cemented to TV programs and videos. Then, slowly weaken the hold. Cut the hours. Search for pleasurable activities, like swimming, nature walks, and court games, to substitute for some of the TV time. Even reading, another "inactivity," can help break TV's grip.

Pounds and Inches

Measuring pounds and inches may upset or please you. By all means, track and record what the scale and tape measure show.

But beware. As said, the scale sometimes lies. To make it more honest, keep it in the same place: Tape the floor surrounding it; draw a line where toes go. Beware also that weight may stick no matter how many snacks and desserts have been denied or basketball games and tennis matches played, because a change in behavior often will not immediately produce a change in weight—actions speak faster than pounds.

Sometimes you will step on the scale, see no loss from the previous week, and still be thinner. You have lost fat and gained lean—a healthy, happy exchange. Punishing yourself by saying something nasty or by feeling like a failure is uncalled for. Indeed, dumping on yourself destroys motivation and self-confidence, not only flattening

Starting weight _____ & ending weight _____
Starting height _____ & ending height _____
Percentile height
for age at start _____ & at end _____
Percentile weight
for age at start _____ & at end _____
Percent overweight
        at start _____ & at end _____
Week 1
Week 2
Week 3
Week 4
Week 5
Week 6
Week 7
Week 8
Week 9
Week 10
Week 11
Week 12
Week 13
Week 14
Week 15
Week 16
Week 17
Week 18
Week 19
Week 20

FIGURE 5.5. Form for tracking weight and overweight.

zest to improve the overweight control program but also pushing you closer to the eating disorders.

Weigh yourself no more than once weekly. Figure 5.5 helps track pounds. Ask the doctor about the height and weight percentiles and about the percents overweight. The figure covers 20 weeks, but perhaps take a year to meet goals.

Beware, too, of the tape measure. After shedding a few pounds, clothes will not always fit better immediately and inches around the middle will not always be fewer suddenly. As well, what you do differently that helps become less overweight does not immediately show up as lost inches—actions speak much faster than inches.

Urges and Thoughts

We have talked about observables—eating, moving, snacking, watching television. These events are public, meaning you and someone else can at the same time watch them unfold. No matter who observes, there are two requirements: behavior happens, people see it happen. If you ride your brother's bike to the corner, you know it and so does everyone else watching you pedal away. If you take three helpings of mashed potato and roast for dinner, you know it and so does everyone else at the table. Many observables are public.

Another kind of observable—the private kind—only you can know of, only you can watch. What you feel compelled to do and what you think about no one but you can witness. Your urges and thoughts are known to you alone.

Urges and thoughts affect actions, and actions affect urges and thoughts. You go downstairs to the family room, turn on the television, see a commercial about some extraordinarily good chocolate, and suddenly want candy.

So you pick out ten or so candy kisses from the filled bowl of delights your family keeps nearby for all to see and enjoy; private urge precedes a potentially public action.

Or, sitting in the family room enjoying a late afternoon soap, you reach into this same nearby candy bowl and take out a few treats. You do not think about candy; you just take it from the dish, automatically. Then, after enjoying the sweets, you want more and take more; initial action precedes urge, later actions follow urge. Possibly, instead of wanting more, maybe besides wanting more, you call yourself weak and worthless; taking candy precedes self-punishing thoughts.

To conquer urges to eat the wrong foods at the wrong times, to stop self-disparaging thoughts sapping motivation and self-worth, and to overcome actions spawning unwanted urges and thoughts or resulting from them, know yourself. Track and catch urges to snack. Track and catch thoughts about yourself.

Eating, Activity, Feelings

Gauge feelings about your looks, control, power, intelligence, strength, happiness. Tally how long during the day you played sedentary games and watched television and how long you ran, swam, biked, skated. Also, check whether you bused or walked to school today. Walking is one of the simplest yet best ways to exercise. Says esteemed pediatrician Dr. Platon Collipp in *Childhood Obesity:*

> Physical activities . . . that can be done alone or with a minimum of others should be taught to obese children . . . Walking or hiking would seem to be the best . . . (p. 330)[10]

Moreover, look closely at your eating, and determine whether you ate sensibly, felt in control, and said no to high-fat foods.

Figure 5.6 helps you comprehensively appraise your day's eating, exercising, feelings. Total not only minutes spent doing sit-down and move-about activities but also positive and negative statements about eating and feelings.

Day & date _____

Place an "X" before each statement that applies to you.

My Activities Today

(In your answers, if today is a school day, consider only the times before and after school, including evening. If it's not a school day, consider the whole day.)

Sit-down activities other than watching TV (playing cards or similar games, reading, studying, talking on the telephone, etc.)

1. None today (no more than a minute)
2. An hour or less (but more than a minute)
3. More than one hour (but less than two hours)
4. More than two hours (but less than three hours)
5. More than three hours
    Total minutes for sit-downs =

Watching television
1. None today (no more than a minute)

FIGURE 5.6. Form to appraise eating, activity, and feelings. Ideas for some of the items for the section "My Feelings Today" have come from Fitts, W. H. (1964). *Tennessee Self Concept Scale.* Nashville: Counselor Recordings and Tests.

2. An hour or less (but more than a minute)
3. More than one hour (but less than two hours)
4. More than two hours (but less than three hours)
5. More than three hours (but less than four hours)
6. More than four hours (but less than five hours)
7. More than five hours (but less than six hours)
8. More than six hours
   Total minutes for TV =

Energetic activities (running, jogging, biking, swimming, tennis, cross-country skiing, dancing, etc.)
6. None today (no more than a minute)
7. 30 minutes or less (but more than a minute)
8. More than 30 minutes (but less than one hour)
9. More than one hour (but less than two hours)
10. More than two hours
   Total minutes for energetics =

Walking
11. None today (no more than a minute)
12. Walked 20 minutes or less (but more than a minute)
13. Walked more than 20 minutes (but less than one hour)
14. Walked more than one hour
   Total minutes for walking =

Cars or buses
15. Spent no time in either today
16. Spent 30 minutes or less (but something) in either today
17. Spent more than 30 minutes in either
   Total minutes in car and on bus =

FIGURE 5.6. *Continued*

My Eating Today

1. Today I overate
2. Today I did not overeat
3. Today, while at home, I ate in places other than the living room or dining room
4. Today I ate what I had planned to
5. Today I ate too little
6. Today I vomited after eating
7. Today I feel good about how much I ate
8. Today I feel bad about how much I ate
9. Today all I ate was fast-foods
10. Today I'm in control of my eating
11. Today I bought numerous snack foods
12. Today I ate numerous snack foods
13. Today I substituted vegetables and/or fruit for snack foods
14. Today I ate sensibly
15. Today I did not eat sensibly
16. Today I refused some high-fat foods

(Positives are 2, 4, 7, 10, 13, 14, 16)
   Total positives checked =
(Negatives are 1, 3, 5, 6, 8, 9, 11, 12, 15)
   Total negatives checked =

My Feelings Today

1. Today I feel I have a healthy body
2. Today I feel I am a nobody
3. Today I feel good about myself
4. Today I feel I am unsociable
5. Today I feel I am satisfied to be just who I am

FIGURE 5.6. *Continued*

6. Today I feel I was as sociable as I wanted to be
7. Today I feel I have an unhealthy body
8. Today I feel I tried to be somewhat careful about my appearance
9. Today I feel unloved by my family
10. Today I feel ugly
11. Today I feel smart
12. Today I did not feel I was the person I wanted to be
13. Today I feel I liked my looks
14. Today I feel inadequate socially
15. Today I feel I got along fine with others
16. Today I feel I was unfriendly
17. Today I feel I have little control over what happens to me
18. Today I feel afraid
19. Today I feel strong
20. Today I feel sloppy
21. Today I feel clean
22. Today I feel dumb
23. Today I feel I have willpower
24. Today I feel self-conscious
25. Today I feel happy
26. Today I feel I have weak willpower or none at all
27. Today I feel repulsive to myself
28. Today I feel I have lots of control over what happens to me
29. Today I feel lonely

(Positives are 1, 3, 5, 6, 8, 11, 13, 15, 19, 21, 23, 25, 28)

Total positives checked =

(Negatives are 2, 4, 7, 9, 10, 12, 14, 16, 17, 18, 20, 22, 24, 26, 27, 29)

Total negatives checked =

FIGURE 5.6. *Continued*

Teenagers in our clinic find this recording form eye-opening.

Chapter 5 says learn about what you eat, do, think, and feel. It also says track pounds and inches; as will be shown, there is yet more to track. The overriding message has been that learning about yourself helps you take charge of yourself. The next chapter carries forward this idea as it reveals ways to bring about change.

CHAPTER **6**

TEENS IN CHARGE ———————
USING POSITIVES

To eat better and move more, change the way you live. To make that change, build up behaviors that promote thinning and tear down those preventing it, topics to which we turn.

BRING IN POSITIVES

Socrates said most of us eat to live, but some of us live to eat. No matter into which group you fall, eating is still behavior. We all eat: if too little, we emaciate ourselves; if too much, we fatten ourselves.

Coming home after a hard day at school, having had half a lunch and no breakfast, you fling open the refrigerator door and see a slice of peach cobbler leftover from last night's dessert. It beckons you. Knowing this is about the best-tasting fat and carbohydrate combination in the Western world, you take it, eat it, love it. That it tastes good is a positive of eating it; later to come are the positives of feeling relaxed and feeling satisfied. On the other hand, if you hate the cobbler, you have experienced a negative.

Positives and negatives control actions. If a certain food gratifies, you will again eat it. If it dissatisfies, you probably will not: Overeat chocolate-covered peanuts and get sick, and you will perhaps never let another chocolate nut near your lips. Positives and negatives influence eating. How they influence your eating tells much about how you and food relate: If eating even just a bit more than a cat does makes you anxious, you may starve, as does the anorexic who fears fatness; if eating eases the pain of rejection and the stresses of living, you may binge, as do many teenagers and adults.

Positives and negatives follow behavior. Though they cannot affect what's already happened, they can and do affect the future, for a positive increases the chance that behavior like that originally leading to the positive will recur. If one night you enjoy four slices of roast beef for dinner, you will likely again have this kind of meal. Positives make the behavior that results in them more probable, more likely to happen again and again.

I want students in the classes I teach on obesity to ask questions, so when they raise their hands I call on them and try to respond kindly and informatively. My calling on them and reacting nicely are positives for them that make their asking questions comfortable, fulfilling, valuable. I hope.

Like most people, I have bad days. If a student asks a question and I show my worst side, "We've already talked about that. What's your problem? Can't you pay attention?", I would be punishing what I want to reward, weakening what I want to strengthen. The questioner would think I am a jerk and so would the rest of the class. In the future, there would be fewer questions, possibly many absences.

If you want Alice or John to greet you each day, answer their "hellos" with your own. If you want top grades on an upcoming test, yet find daily studying intolerable, make a daily hour or so of it pay off immediately: give yourself $5, a nice lunch or dinner, a new video . . .

for studying. Attach positives to behavior to strengthen behavior.

Bringing in Positives to Help a Girl of Fourteen

Over 20 years ago, Dr. Richard Foxx of Pennsylvania State reported using the simple method of giving positives in order to help an overweight retarded teenager living in a place much like a hospital.[1] Before getting positives, this 5 foot 3 inch girl weighed about 240 pounds. After six months, still before getting positives, she had lost roughly 23 pounds. But she needed to lose more.

Attempting to learn what for her would be a powerful positive, Dr. Foxx discovered that she enjoyed chatting with him at the residence canteen. So, when the girl lost weight, she and Dr. Foxx would go together to the canteen and talk; they did this during the afternoon, once a week, soon after the weekly check on weight.

The girl knew the rules of this game—lose weight, have chat—but how she won at it I do not know. Possibly, she breakfasted on plain cereal with skim milk and no sugar, lunched on salads, avoided desserts, walked more, rode a bike, exercised at a gym. It was up to her to choose foods and exercises. Dr. Foxx did not say how to lose weight, did not change critical behaviors leading to losing weight. He just arranged things so that she got positives when she did lose weight.

And she did. She took off nearly 79 pounds in 40 weeks (usually teenagers do not lose so much so fast), a rate of almost two pounds a week. But we do not know if she lost unhealthily: if she fasted, eliminated essential macronutrients, vomited before weight-checks. The problem of a weight-loss focus, an exclusively weight-loss focus, as was done here, is failing to zero in on behaviors essential to it.

Possibly, this illustration offends you because it appears Dr. Foxx bribed his patient. But did he really? He paid her with something she liked and valued for doing something he thought good for her. If you call paying and praising bribing, you denigrate the acceptable and customary: Teachers grade their students, parents praise their children, bosses pay their employees. Systematically, precisely, and consistently giving positives for behaviors has been and continues to be done. You would be angry if the policy stopped, if your boss decreed that no longer will you be paid for work.

Calling all positives bribes is wrong. *The American Heritage Dictionary* defines a bribe as "something, such as money, offered or given to induce or influence a person to act dishonestly."[2] Bribery perverts judgment, corrupts conduct. Your boss does not do that when she awards you a Christmas bonus. Your history teacher does not do that when he marks A+ on your well-done term paper. On the contrary, you are being rewarded for good acts.

When he went to the canteen and talked with his patient, Dr. Foxx rewarded; he did not bribe. You are not bribing when you give yourself positives for behaving in ways that help you lose overweight. In time, you will no longer need the special positives like money; potent and enduring feelings of accomplishment arising from your victorious struggles will replace them.

Bringing in Positives after School

Harassed at school for being heavy, 16-year-old Alycen nonetheless is popular. She has friends and often socializes with them. One place her group congregates after school is the nearby coffeeshop. While there, Alycen plans events and cements ties. It is there, however, she finds controlling eating difficult. Wanting to be thinner, she has this conflict: If she watches her eating, she will be ridiculed because watching admits to a problem, and her friends, intolerant of differences, will tease her; but, if she eats richly, she gains and risks more ridicule for getting heavier. Alycen is betwixt and between.

Alycen knows eating better may draw unwanted attention, but thinks it worse to grow heavier. So, she decides to regulate snacking at the coffeeshop, yet cautiously, trying not by her actions to advertise overweight control. She looks for appetizing snacks that do not, by their presence, scream, "Guess who's trying to be thin?"

By snacking better, she hopes to trim down. Echoing the family doctor, her parents say for her to keep to present weight and grow taller to erase chubbiness. Toward this end, Alycen brings in positives. To snack better, she needs to know what the coffeeshop offers. Armed with a calorie and fat-gram counter, she scrutinizes the restaurant menu, defining acceptable snacks as those of 300 or less calories and low in fat and discovering that a lightly buttered baked potato or dish of fruit qualify. But the mammoth pecan roll dripping butter, apple pie smothered in ice cream, and hot fudge sundae are out.

After cataloguing options, she develops a way to track choices and reward successes. Alycen will mentally note what snack she orders and then later, at home, record her selections. Also, she will reward herself with the money saved from her frugal eating, using accumulated funds to purchase a new sweater. Positives, money for the sweater and feeling triumph over her dilemma, fortify her resolve.

Bringing in positives is a simple tactic for overcoming overweight; give yourself something for doing something;

you define both somethings. But there is more to consider, for you must not only pick the right behaviors and positives but also apply the positives carefully.

Bring in Strong Positives

If you love movies, use them as positives. Say you want to snack more on apples and less on peanut butter cookies, walk to school daily, and keep more detailed records of eating and exercising. Tie these behaviors to movies: Do the deeds, get the shows.

Overweight since the sixth grade and now, five years later, still overweight, you decide to reduce and so search for strong positives. Wanting many things, you thrill at the thought of having grandmother's nine-year-old mint-condition Ford; she is willing to part with it for a pittance, all but $200 of which you have. Asking parents to help, you strike a deal: for each lost pound, they agree to give you $20. Quite a deal.

The problem with it, a problem like Dr. Foxx had in his treatment for the 14-year-old, is that losing weight is your only way to the positive. When the positive is strong and losing pou..ds is the road to it, the only road to it, you might act unhealthily to get it. Fasting all day Thursday to be a pound less on Friday morning and therefore $20 richer is not how to earn a strong positive. Attach positives to wholesome changes: eating lower-in-fat foods, walking, playing team sports.

Be Clear about Behaviors and Payoffs

Plan what gets what. Agree ahead that having an apple and two cookies instead of the usual ten cookies earns the show. Before beginning overweight control, write what the positive is and exactly what gets it.

Be Consistent and Immediate

Each time you behave as wanted, bring in right away the planned positive.

But there is a technical problem in being consistent and immediate. Some strong positives cannot be used repeatedly and promptly. You snack better at 4:00 P.M. Monday, but cannot go to the show until 9:00 P.M. Friday. Maybe waiting is not a problem for you, but rewarding many snacking improvements will soon exhaust the available movies.

There is a simple solution. Give yourself points for each improvement. Each better snack, say, nets 10 points, and accumulating 50 earns you the movie. Points build progress.

Another plus to points, to be redeemed for tangible positives, is that they allow paying more later when things get tougher. In time, keeping data, exercising more, and so on, decline in attractiveness. If later in the program you have lost some of your motivation, renew it by giving yourself more points for the same improvements. If each instance of playing an active game during the first week leads to 10 points, pay off 15 points during the twelfth week.

Still another advantage of points is they add variety to the overweight control program. Let points buy movies, trips to the mall, new clothes, new runners, and more. Variety reduces tedium.

Where and What Are the Positives?

Positives are everywhere—at home, at school, at malls, to name only some places. Positives may be a new tennis racket, a trip to the beauty salon, a new football, a concert, a kind word from mother or father, a computer game, a vacation from your brother, a jelly doughnut, a four-figure bank account, a time to be alone. Options abound.

But what for you is a positive may not be for your best friend; it may even be a negative for him. You like board games; he hates them. And what for you is a positive under today's noon sun may disappear by the time it sets.

Some positives, however, stay strong and please most of us. Money typifies. Owning a fistful of $1000 bills would excite most of us today, tomorrow, and if we still had any left, next year. Approval is another powerful, lasting positive. Years before you found out what money bought, you sought approval. Probably those taking care of you during your earliest days, when still in diapers you lay in your crib, ministered to you, smiling and speaking gently as they did so. From their service and kindness, you came to love attention and praise. And you still do, even though today you earn them differently from how you did long ago and differently from how you will in years to come.

Dr. Joseph Cautela of the Behavior Therapy Institute in Massachusetts and colleagues have published lists of positives to stir the interests of most teenagers.[3] On these lists are movies, concerts, sporting events, clothes, sports equipment, and more. Table 6.1 names several classes of positives and identifies examples within each class.

Remember when using activities or tangibles, consider giving points: Save them up, cash them in.

Foods and Drinks

The table includes them, but as the late eminent psychiatrist Dr. Hilde Bruch cautions, consumables attach to

TABLE 6.1. Possible Positives[a,b]

Commodities

Baseball equipment
Basketball equipment
Clothes and shoes
Football equipment
CD player
Car accessories
Money toward car
Computer
Computer program
Computer equipment
Video game equipment
Video games
Board games
Books (paper, hard)
Magazine subscription
Magazines
Money
Perfume
Cologne
Stereo equipment
Tape deck
Boom box
Caligraphy equipment
New clothes
Posters
Paintings

Activities

Going to movie
Going shopping
Learning to keyboard
Going to concert
Going to game (all sports)
Trip with parents
Trip alone
Trip with friends
Woodworking
Family bike outing
Getting hair done
Going to restaurant of choice
Going swimming
Giving a party

Consumables

Eclair
Candy
Fast food
Soft drink
Doughnut
Ice cream
Popcorn

[a]Build from this list, which only samples available positives, your own personal menu of positives. Attempt to earn positives outright or by accumulating points toward their purchase.
[b]Sources: Cautela, J. R. (1981). *Behavior Analysis Forms for Clinical Intervention*, Vol. 2. Champaign: Research Press. LeBow, M. D. (1991). *Overweight Children*. New York: Insight Books.

emotions as well as to hunger.[4] Making sugary soft drinks, doughnuts, and candy bars positives in effect says behaviors should lead to fun food. But if you fight the urges to eat that well up within you when happy, sad, angry, and bored, say instead that behaviors controlling overweight should lead to movies, clothes, and praise.

As positives, foods and drinks may not only convey the wrong message but also compromise progress. If you argue that six doughnuts on the weekend is a right and fitting consequence to cutting down high-fat snacks during the week, you forget that possibly the calories and grams of fat allowed on Saturday and Sunday exceed those prevented Monday through Friday.

Progress

To control overweight, control behavior. Attach positives to healthy changes in actions. Eat better, move more. When you do, award yourself points toward something you want. Activities, commodities, and (if used carefully) consumables strengthen the behaviors that control overweight.

But so also, as mentioned, does knowing that things are working. Seeing progress lifts the spirit.

Positives: A Menu, a Kind Word, and a Friend

Table 6.1 only samples the positives out there. Anything that seems to be a positive is a positive as long as the behavior obtaining it strengthens. Construct a list, a menu, of likes. And remember: preferences change quickly, often faster than overweight does. Seek variety.

As well, praise yourself for earning the points or tangible positive. Suppose you award yourself five points toward the twenty required to see this year's Academy Award–winning picture. You net the five by walking rather than busing to your best friend's house. Just before you knock on his door, praise your triumph. To yourself say, "Actually, the walk wasn't bad. I know I can do what I want. Little by little, I'm taking charge. I'm doing well."

Add to the power of activity-positives by enjoying them with other people. The movie may be even more of a positive if you go to it with a few friends.

When bringing in positives, remember this:

- Find your positives. Consult Table 6.1.
- Create a menu of positives.
- Say what positives you will use.
- Use strong positives.
- Define precisely the behaviors to strengthen, the behaviors to which you will attach positives.
- Deliver positives consistently and, when possible, immediately.
- For outings, trips, fun activities, and many other positives, use points. Award, save up, and cash in points for the positives.
- Track success.
- Praise success.
- Be careful, when using food and drink, not to compromise progress or let emotions rule your eating.

If the tactic of bringing in positives fails, check that you are following these guidelines or combine the tactic with another this book describes. What's more, consider again if overweight control is right for you now.

WEAKENING BEHAVIORS

It's 4:00 P.M. Tired and hungry after another day of high school, you head home past the local bakery and its irresistible window display of newly baked pastries. Their smell, detectable and delectable even through glass, captures you; saliva of want fills your mouth. Seeing them, especially chocolate eclairs with whipped cream insides spilling onto flaky chocolate-laden crusts, captivates you— impossible to pass up. Aware that chocolate eclairs have more calories and grams of fat than the moon has rocks, you nonetheless stride into the store, buy one, down it in five bites, and walk the block home. This sequence repeats daily throughout the week.

Trying to interrupt rapid gaining, you know eclairs destroy goals by adding fat calories and, worse, by draining motivation. You could find another path home, have an apple ready to eat on the walk, allow eclairs (some of the time). Whatever, weaken the hold the bakery has on you. The next three tactics, which disrupt unwanted behaviors, show what to do. As with bringing in positives, think of each of them as ingredients of an overweight control recipe; none is the whole recipe.

Taking Away Positives

This procedure is often called response–cost; it makes the response, the behavior, cost. Wanting a VCR, you save up birthday money, two months of baby-sitting money, and three months of lawn-mowing money. Now, reasonably well off, you nonetheless postpone buying the video equipment. You want more to control overweight, an essential part of which is limiting yourself to one eclair a week—to be purchased Fridays.

Put twenty $5 bills in a jar on your dresser. Each day, except Friday, you go to the bakery and buy a treat, remove a $5 bill and donate it to someone in your family— maybe little brother. Make the behavior you want to weaken, cost; take away positives.

"Are you kidding?" you say. "Who'd do that?"

My answer: someone who wants to lessen high-calorie, high-fat between-meal eating and who finds other tactics fail. You have to want what response–cost promises. Include this maneuver in a program that relies on managing yet more of your eating, increasing your exercise, assessing fat calories, bringing in positives.

Attempting such a broader approach, psychologist Dr. William DiScipio and colleagues blended several tactics to treat six overweight, emotionally disturbed, hospitalized teenage girls.[5] At the start, these 13- to 16-year-olds weighed from about 165 pounds to nearly 208 pounds. All had gained since coming to the hospital—one almost 95 pounds.

The girls volunteered for overweight therapy, which for some lasted up to four months. Trying to avoid conditions for teasing, Dr. DiScipio had his patients eat the foods of the hospital, not special menus, just less at meals and snacks. To help the girls eat better, the therapists brought in positives, conducted group therapy, and took away positives.

Losing weight earned money, $1 a pound up to 5 pounds and, thereafter, 50 cents per pound. Since losing is harder later, paying less later is curious; as would be expected, the girls lost best at the start. The second tactic, group therapy, occurred in 40- to 50-minute meetings. Taking away positives, the third tactic, amounted to fining each teen each time for having candy, sugary soft drinks, seconds at meals, and other actions compromising over-weight control.

Although taking away positives had no remarkable impact, results revealed that the teenager doing the best (fined infrequently) lost about 26 pounds. Her friend (doing the worst) put on about ½ pound. The four other girls lost from ½ pound to 13 pounds.

To make responses cost, do this:

- Define and keep records of the behavior you do not want—the behavior to weaken.
- Set aside positives (e.g., money) to give away if you behave as you do not want.

Substituting Behavior

If idle hands are the Devil's workshop, that's because trouble is hard to stay away from . . . if you've nothing to do instead. Quibble with this logic if you wish, but data do argue that to weaken something, do something else. The next two tactics apply this idea to the food world. They say find behaviors to do in place of those you no longer want as habits. In a word, substitute.

Applying this reasoning years ago, in what is now called a landmark project, Dr. Richard Stuart of the University of Washington taught eight heavy women weighing between 172 and 224 pounds self-control.[6] Under his guidance, the women substituted in order to control urges to eat between meals. First, they searched for, found, and listed behaviors they liked other than snacking. Then, when they had urges to snack, they did these other competing behaviors—they substituted. They embedded in a comprehensive program of care doing something pleasurable rather than doing something fattening, and as a result two of the women lost more than 25 pounds, three nearly 36 pounds, and three over 45 pounds.

Try substitution:

- Search for enjoyable activities, and list these substitutes. Possibly you like telephoning a friend, reading a magazine, painting, watching a show on television, playing a computer game.
- Post the list in your room or wherever you can easily find it.
- When cravings to eat high-fat food strike, consult the list and substitute. Save the substitutes for times you will need them.
- Bring in positives for successes.
- Praise successes.

By bringing in positives, including praise and points toward some purchase or fun outing, you strengthen the procedure of substitution. The progress you will see will strengthen it even more.

Unnamed Substitutions

Substitution will help many of you remove obstacles on the bumpy road to controlling overweight. But if you cannot predict substitutes, just give yourself positives when you avoid doing what you wish to no longer do. Suppose you want to snack less after dinner. Typically, you snack at about 7:00, 8:00, and 9:00. By knowing when you snack and by arranging that points buy positives for less snacking, you can work the method of unnamed substitutions.

You want a pool table. Your parents agree to buy it once you earn 1000 points, points for longer and longer snack-free intervals (or snack-better episodes) during the evening. For illustration, consider the snack-free case. Plan a 6:30 P.M. snack. Try to avoid unscheduled eating until 7:30 P.M., and if successful, give yourself one point. For every 10 minutes beyond 7:30 P.M. you do not snack, provided there has been no more than one snack following dinner (the planned 6:30 P.M. snack), give yourself another point. Avoiding unscheduled eating until 8:00 P.M. earns you four points—one for reaching 7:30 and three more for reaching 8:00. Give bonuses, five extra points, for doing especially well, such as making it to 8:30. Not snacking until 9:00, except once at 6:30, gets you a total of 15 points. Your successes grow, your points grow, and (as the pool table nears) your motivation grows.

Take these steps:

- For a week or so, observe and record when you snack or when specifically you snack on high-fat foods.
- Create a menu of positives.
- Decide how many points buys each positive.
- At those times you would have snacked poorly but now do not snack at all or snack on low-fat foods, award yourself points.
- Decide how many points each triumph earns.
- Decide how bonuses are earned.
- Resist making points too easy to get.
- Resist making points too hard to get.
- Plan when to cash in points and for what.
- Praise successes.

The tactics of named and unnamed substitution superimpose acceptable behavior on unacceptable behavior and by so doing weaken the unacceptable behavior. With the help of your parents and doctor, you decide what is acceptable and unacceptable. By substituting, you weaken behavior without punishing it, giving to yourself rather than taking away from yourself.

The promise of this chapter, by naming, explaining, and exemplifying the use of positives to strengthen and weaken behavior, is that much can be done to control overweight. The next chapter also proposes rational effective remedies, but those it describes, which often use positives, are more intricate.

CHAPTER 7

TEENS IN CHARGE ———————

THINKING, REARRANGING, CONTRACTING, AND ASSERTING TO CONTROL OVERWEIGHT

Most of the forenamed principles and tactics for controlling overweight are enriched and strengthened here, as we discuss tactics involving thoughts, the environment, agreements, and actions.

THINKING CONSTRUCTIVELY

If you think you are no more than a slug, you will meet the world downcast, expect little from what you do, avoid challenges and hurdles. Instead, if you think well of yourself, you will meet the world straight on, feel confident, and behave confidently, confronting trials and tackling obstacles.

To find out what you think of and say to yourself, listen to yourself. Eavesdrop on what you tell yourself throughout the day as you face your world and respond to it. I suggested (Chapter 5) tracking thoughts, the substance of your private world, because thoughts and self-statements affect actions. To help control overweight, catch self-talk and thoughts.

The positive that goes on in your mind enlivens, the negative dampens, sucking dry your motivation to forge ahead. Indeed, negative thinking may so upset you that you become the slave of denial, purging, and bingeing. About overeating after hurtful thinking, psychologists Drs. Michael and Katherine Mahoney warn in *Permanent Weight Control* that nasty self-talk about violating a rigid diet-standard will for some soon produce a binge.[1]

You say to yourself, *Nothing will make me thinner except starving or vomiting.* Such negative thinking may so upset you that a slip becomes a catastrophe. Negative thinking begins soon after you, zealous to control overweight, make unrealistic promises:

- *Never again will my lips touch a doughnut,* and you love doughnuts.
- *Never again will I spend an evening in front of the TV,* and you need to escape, sometimes.
- *Never again will I dine out,* and you enjoy the spontaneously arranged dinners out with your family.
- *Never again will I go to the coffeeshop, even if all my friends go there,* and you want to stay popular.
- *Never again will I get an ice cream cone, even if it's hot outside,* and you know such summer delights make hot days bearable.
- *Never again will I eat birthday cake,* and you realize the opportunities to have this tasty symbol of annual passage equal the number of friends you have.

"Never agains" never last. They are not only temporary but also trouble, for when you slip from overweight control, as most do now and then, you likely will attack your character:

> *I'm too weak-willed; after all, I wouldn't be overweight if I wasn't weak.*

Talking to yourself against yourself sabotages yourself and makes you feel worthless. Talk to yourself in support of yourself, and challenge the scurrilous thoughts. You have an unplanned-for treat and think:

> *I have no willpower when it comes to pie, cake, and doughnuts. There's no sense in trying to trim down. I'm fat and ugly and I'll always be fat and ugly.*

Challenge the thought:

> *I do love pies, cakes, and doughnuts. I can have them sometimes. No matter how overweight I am, I'm not ugly. If I choose to be thinner, and do so healthfully, I do so because I want to, not because my friends say to. I'm in charge of what I do and don't do.*

You are embarrassed to exercise and think:

> *I can't shoot baskets—one of my friends will see me and laugh.*

As Dr. Kirschenbaum and his associates say, combat the thought.[2]

> *Exercise is important for me right now. I don't particularly want anybody to see me, but I'm not going to deny myself*

the opportunity to exercise. The V-shapes don't own the courts. I need to exercise, and I will.

You feel that a drastic measure is needed:

I'm a pig when I get around food. The only way to lose is to starve.

Challenge the thought and be constructive:

I do love to eat. But so do most people. I'm not a pig, I'm a person. I don't have to starve to control. There are things I can do that will help me deal better with food. I'll treat myself rationally and healthily.

Use a diary to record thoughts and the challenges to them you make. Set aside a few pages, dividing each into three columns: circumstance, negative thought, constructive (positive, better) thought. University of Pennsylvania psychiatrist Dr. Aaron Beck and colleagues have developed a more elaborate form of this strategy to help their depressed patients catch and challenge destructive thoughts and by so doing feel better. In *Cognitive Therapy of Depression,* a classic in the field of treating depression, the authors write,

Recording cognitions and responses in parallel columns is a way to begin examining, evaluating, and modifying cognitions. The patient is instructed to write his cognitions in one column and then to write a "reasonable response" to the cognitions in the next column. (p. 163)[3]

Sometimes a negative thought goes by so fast that all that's left is a bad feeling. Ask yourself what occurred before the feeling, what was the situation, what were others doing, what were others saying. Then, re-create the destructive thought. Following this, challenge it: Think better—more constructively, more logically, more positively.

To think better of yourself and talk better to yourself, try the following:

- Divide each of several diary pages into three columns: circumstance, negative thought, constructive thought.
- When you feel bad, write what has just happened—circumstance.
- Then write what you are thinking and saying—negative thought.
- If you cannot decode the negative thought, ask yourself about a constructive way to handle the circumstance. Write your conclusion in column three.
- If you can decipher the negative thought, challenge it by writing in column three a constructive, logical, positive alternative.
- Study what you have done. Praise yourself for doing this exercise, maybe award a positive.

REARRANGING YOUR WORLD

Three years ago, two days before the final exam in Abnormal Psychology, a class I teach, a panicked student pounded on my office door. His bloodshot eyes, mussed hair, sweaty brow, and shaky gait attested to his anxiety.

He said, "I want to go to graduate school in Psychology. Please don't think I can't do better than what I'm getting in Abnormal."

"Why not?" I asked. I wasn't being purposely cruel.

"Because I can't seem to study well this term. I just moved into University College [dormitory]. I always fall asleep whenever I study there," he said.

I inquired about his study habits.

"Three days before each of your tests, I try to cram—six hours straight a night. I study after dinner. The library on campus is a zoo in the evening, so I stay in my dorm room. My room's quiet, but the dorm is noisy."

"How is it that you fall asleep? Do you fall asleep at your desk?

"I guess the material makes me nod off. I don't like my desk; the chair's too hard; I study in bed. Why can't I study better?"

He answered his own question: He studies after dinner, probably tired, and where he sleeps; he studies right before a test, tackling large amounts of text in a short period, doing too large a chore in too brief a time. Little wonder he has trouble. To study better, he needs to create conditions for studying better: He needs to study less material for more days, starting before dinner and in a place where he does not sleep. When he creates conditions conducive to the behavior he wants, he has rearranged his world.

Take another example. Wanting to thin down, you watch both what you tell yourself and eat, giving yourself positives for doing things that help control overweight and taking them away for not. Deciding to cut an hour from your usual 5–6 hours a day of television, you free an hour for exercise. But the deal collapses, not because you hate to sacrifice television, but because you fail to create the environment for exercise.

You intend to play an hour of volleyball in the gym after school. Because you keep no sweat clothes at school, you go to the gym dressed the way you typically go to school: snug jeans, snug shirt. Everyone else dresses for exercise. Trying to play, you feel awkward and uncomfortable, perform badly, and decide not to participate again.

The conditions right for studying differ from those right for exercising, but for both, creating correct circumstances involves rearranging the environment. Psychologists call this rearranging and the rearrangement itself Stimulus Control.

Stimulus Control

You are walking down the street when along comes a seemingly free-spirited 25-year-old with purple-colored hair, the top of which he has teased to stand upright. Barefooted, dressed in a red, blue, and green loose-fitting shirt and baggy jeans, he carries on his shoulder an oversized boom box that blasts a driving tune. Though compelled to look long at him, you instead only glance. He is a stimulus. You are dressed more conservatively than he, and no noise radiates from your shoulder area. As he passes, Mr. Purple-hair glances at you. You are a stimulus.

Both of you are stimuli, because each affects the other's behavior—glancing. A stimulus, no matter how compelling, complex, exciting, dull, or strange, is a time, place, person, or event that affects behavior.

Two Kinds of Stimuli: The After and the Before

Recall, stimuli following behavior are "positives" if, because of them, the behavior followed strengthens, occurs again. Stimuli following behavior are the *after* stimuli. You cross the boulevard to get to the other side. Crossing is behavior, the other side is for you now and in the future, provided friends, relatives, and attracting shops remain there, a positive stimulus—an after stimulus.

But there is more to the crossing story. You do not just cross the street; you wait until the light turns green, especially if cars speed down the boulevard. Because the green light precedes safe crossing, it becomes a stimulus *before* behavior—an antecedent of behavior. Your presence is the antecedent of the unusual-looking stranger's glance; his presence is the antecedent of yours. Not only positives and negatives, aftereffects, control behavior, so do antecedents—places, people, thoughts, sights.

If food is your ungiving master, ask about the antecedents of your eating: about where and with whom you are, about time of day, about sight of food, about sight of others enjoying food, about urges and thoughts. Ask about the unwanted connections existing between your world and your eating and about those you would like to see there. Create antecedents for improved eating. Remove antecedents for troublesome eating. Rearrange your world to practice Stimulus Control.

Some Rearrangements to Consider

To Control Exercise

- Have exercise apparel and equipment (e.g., bike) ready.
- Say where you will exercise.
- Say when you will exercise.

- Say what you plan, what you will do if plans change, and who, if anyone, will join you when you exercise.

To Control Eating: General

- Unless you have planned to snack, let urges to eat between meals signal playing a game, telephoning a friend, writing in your diary—something enjoyable (see Chapter 6).
- Ask friends not to pester you to eat high-fat foods.
- Schedule when you will eat.

Home Rearrangements to Control Eating

- Fill your plate in the kitchen if you eat in the dining room.
- Give yourself large enough portions, but not too large.
- Ask that stored leftovers not be easy to grab.
- Designate where to eat, and eat nowhere else.
- Ask parents to stock vegetables and fruits and few ready-to eat foods, to stop telling you to clean your plate, to stock few high-fat foods, to remove candy dishes from the TV room.
- Keep your snacks, except vegetables and fruits, in your own container. Write your name on it.
- Avoid eating while watching TV, while reading, or while listening to music. Eat, but do not accompany it with pleasing distractions.
- Keep no food in your bedroom.

School Rearrangements to Control Eating

- Keep no food in your locker.
- Avoid fatty cafeteria foods. Perhaps, bring your lunch.
- Avoid vending machines.

Restaurant Rearrangements to Control Eating

- Ask servers not to serve bread before the meal.
- Learn the menus of those restaurants you frequent.

Think over which of these stimulus control suggestions suit you. Develop others. Your goals are to disconnect antecedents from unwanted behaviors and to connect antecedents to wanted behaviors.

DESIGNING A CONTRACT

Contracts are agreements. You and someone else each agree to do something. The contract specifies those somethings and that each of you will live up to promises only if the other lives up to promises. To avoid hassles of who-promised-what, most contracts are written; after negotiation, parties sign them. By signing the contract, each person commits to following it. If one fails to live up to its strictures, breaks the contract, parties either forget about the agreement or battle over it in court.

Contracts for thinning are not legally binding; they are only written promises. Once, psychiatrist Dr. Michael Skopec and I contracted with eight overweight adults wanting to reduce. The contracts, signed at Dartmouth Medical School, had 25 clauses each and ran for 53 weeks. Before treatment, patients spent a few days in a hospital, where a physician inspected samples of their fat cells (Chapter 2). The physician determined if these overweight volunteers had excessively large or excessively numerous fat cells, keeping the results to himself until after treatment. We wanted to find out who lost more weight, those with excessively numerous or those with excessively large fat cells.

Six of the contract's clauses, covering the first 13 weeks of treatment, show payment for progress; patients gave us money for treatment and we returned some of it for their losing weight and inches, keeping records, and learning about self-control.

- Clause 1: [I get] One dollar for each pound I lose from my lowest recorded weight.
- Clause 2: [I get] Fifty cents for tabulating what and how much I eat during the week.
- Clause 3: [I get] Fifty cents for tabulating how much I exercise during the week.
- Clause 4: [I get] One dollar and fifty cents for each inch I lose from my waist.
- Clause 5: [I get] Fifty cents for each constructive weight-control suggestion I make.
- Clause 6: [I get] One dollar for passing a quiz on principles of self-control.

During the remaining weeks of the contract, we paid more for each improvement. As behaviors changed, pounds vanished, but whether our patients began the program with numerous or enlarged fat cells did not matter.

They received money, weekly or close to weekly. Dr. Thomas Coates in San Francisco and colleagues paid their considerably younger patients daily.[4] The daily payoff may better suit you. Figure 7.1 pictures another contract.

Parent promises

1. Count and record foods child eats daily
2. Record child's exercise type and approximate duration daily
3. Sign child's point card and send it to school daily
4. Praise child daily for following the 1200-calorie diet
5. Award points to child
   For cooperating = 2 points
   For not nagging = 1 point
   For eating and exercise control
6. Allow child to cash in points for positives

School (principal and teacher) promises

1. Weigh student on Mondays, Wednesdays, and Fridays
2. Record weights at the weight checks
3. Award points to student:
   $\frac{1}{2}$ pound loss = 10 points
   Bringing in data sheet from home = 10 points
4. Send note to student's parents on Fridays that mentions the following:
   The student's weight that day
   How much weight has changed during the week
   Total points spent at school for the week
   Total points saved in bank account during the week

Student promises

1. Eat only those foods on the 1200-calorie diet provided = 10 points
2. Exercise as planned = 10 points
3. Take note home from school each Friday = 5 points

FIGURE 7.1 Contract for the retarded.

Four people—a principal, a teacher, a parent, and a re-tarded young adult—signed it.

With a contract, you can pledge to reduce or simply not to gain, to change behavior, to bring in positives, to take away positives, to keep records of foods and exercises, to track self-talk, to rearrange your world, or to do most of these and other things.

Avoid narrow contracts, those where promises to reduce combine with giving and removing positives, and nothing else is promised. Focus on behaviors as well as or instead of on losses. The best contracts help you avoid the bakeshop after school, choose more vegetables and less cookies to snack on, break connections between watching television and eating; they also help you choose volleyball, basketball, racquetball, or swimming instead of television, checkers, or other sit-down games. The best contracts target behavior and by so doing help you live a newer way. They focus not only on the behaviors and situations that are problems for you but also on the commodities and activities that are positives for you. The best contracts fit with your needs and preferences and let you pick what and how to change.

Contracts for Teenagers

Laura wanted to be thinner. She did so not because she was maligned for being heavy, although sometimes a friend would anger her by saying she would be prettier if 20 pounds lighter, but because she wanted to feel better in her clothes. Recently 17, she began overweight control at a height of 5 feet 6 inches and weight of 160 pounds. After discussing her plan with her parents and family physician and before attempting change, Laura observed herself (used Figures 5.1 and 5.4) for two weeks. Inspecting data, she learned that she often snacked on candy kisses from a candy dish in the TV room and on potato chips. As well, she learned that she rarely exercised, preferring TV soaps and quiz shows to sports and walking.

To change, Laura resolved to snack less on chips and candy, to keep her daily intake between 1900 and 1950 calories, to play team sports four afternoons each week after school, and (though still driving to school daily) to walk short distances, such as from home to the mailbox. For improving, she vowed to give herself points backed up by new clothes, the money for which she had saved from jobs and presents. Laura framed her ideas into the one-person contract of Figure 7.2.

Notice how Laura blocks losing rapidly, unheathily, mysteriously:

- She gives herself points for small losses ($\frac{1}{2}$ pound a week, no more).
- She allows herself six months to reduce 10 pounds.
- She removes points for deep cuts in calories (fines fasting and going below 1900 calories a day).
- She emphasizes changing behavior (more exercise, less snacking, more record keeping) instead of just losing pounds, even giving herself bonuses for some of the behavior changes.

Notice also that to reach her goals, she specifies methods (e.g., bringing in and taking away positives), and that to uphold the contract, she promises to purchase only

Promises and payoffs to me

Lose weight

Each $\frac{1}{2}$ pound loss = 2 points; I'll check weekly. No more than 2 points can be earned each week by losing weight.

Keep daily calorie intake during the week between 1900 and 1950 = 2 points

Failing to keep daily calories at a minimum of 1900 a day for two or more days loses 2 points

Fasting one or more days loses 20 points

Snack on potato chips ($\frac{1}{2}$ bag) no more than once during the week = 3 points

No snacking on candy kisses during the week = 1 point

No snacking while watching television during the week, unless the snack consists of vegetables = 3 points

Play basketball or badminton in gym for 1 hour or more = 1 point each time

Bonus points: playing basketball or badminton four times (at least 1 hour each time) during the week = 3 points

Each time walk 10 minutes or more = 1 point

Seven days of keeping daily records of changes and point earnings in diary = 2 points

Goals

Lose 10 pounds

Take in 1900 to 1950 calories per day

Reduce snacking on potato chips to no more than once a week

Eliminate snacking on candy kisses

Eliminate snacking, except on vegetables, while watching television

FIGURE 7.2. My contract.

Increase exercise by playing basketball or badminton after school four times or more each week

Increase walking

Ways to help reach goals

Remove candy dish from den (OK with mom. She'll keep candy out of sight)

Have supply of cut vegetables in refrigerator

Buy a container to hold $\frac{1}{2}$ bag of potato chips and put my name on the container

Award myself points to be exchanged for new clothes for behavior changes (playing basketball, badminton, walking, reducing high-calorie snacking while watching TV, snacking less on potato chips, eliminating snacking on candy kisses)

Award myself points for losing weight

Keep runners, clean sweat pants, sweat shirt, badminton racket, and two or three shuttlecocks at school

Arrange with Jen, Sal, Julie, Jeri, and Marci to play basketball with their group on Monday, Wednesday, Thursday, and Friday or play badminton with Marci any of these days

Points buy

25 = white blouse

35 = new runners

50 = new boots

25 = black stirrup pants

25 = teal green ribbed-neck tunic

28 = lined jeans

24 = regular jeans

25 = silk turtleneck

Figure 7.2. *Continued*

50 = Irish wool sweater
40 = lamb's-wool sweater
25 = rugby shirt
40 = warm-up suit
20 = lamb's-wool scarf
20 = pink sleep-shirt
30 = denim front-wrap skirt
40 = gray cardigan
    Cash in points monthly
    Option to cash in points later

Financing the contract

I'll use money from my birthday, Christmas, weekly allowance, and baby-sitting. For the duration of this contract, I'll buy clothes only if I earn points for them

Contracts ends or renegotiated

After 10 pounds lost or after 24 weeks, whichever occurs first

I agree to do my best to live up to this contract.
Signature: ——————————— Date: ——————

Figure 7.2. *Continued*

the new clothes she earns. Laura calculates she could net over 500 points. For example:

- 40 points from losing 10 pounds—2 points per $\frac{1}{2}$ pound
- 48 points from keeping daily calories between 1900 and 1950—2 points a week for 24 weeks
- 30 points from walking 30 times during the contract

- 96 points from playing basketball or badminton four times a week for 24 weeks (1 point per session) plus 72 bonus points—3 per week for 24 weeks

She assigns a portion of the points to each garment based on its actual cost and how much she wants it.

Laura could have contracted with her parents, giving them roles to fill, such as financing the contract, planning (with her) more nutritious meals, planning family exercises.

Contract do's:

- *Write down clauses.*
- *Sign the contract.* All parties to the contract, even if it is only you who contract, should sign it.
- *Spell out the promises.*

Will you keep records of the foods eaten and exercises done?

Will you plan a more nutritious diet?

Will you eat breakfast and lunch?

Will your parents finance the contract?

Will your parents administer positives and remove them or will you?

Is your goal to lose fat (inches) and pounds? (About pounds, if you target weight loss and are not still growing, avoid giving yourself positives for losing the same weight twice or more. Suppose you are 175 pounds, drop to 174, and award yourself a positive. One week later, you are 175 pounds again and so forfeit a positive. You must now lose to 173 pounds, a new low, to earn another positive; once before you were at 174 and got a positive, so you should not get one for being there again.)

- *When writing terms of the contract, specify what actions earn positives and what actions lose them.*
  Does each instance of nasty self-talk result in a fine?
  Will only a 20-minute or greater walk after dinner earn points and no change a fine?
  Could a 20-minute or greater family bike ride substitute for the walk?
  Does each instance of constructive self-talk get you one, five, or ten points?
  Does fasting to lose weight cost ten, twenty, or thirty points?
  Does dropping below 1800 calories per day for two days during the week cost twenty points?
- *Say what each person signing the contract gets for living up to the contract and loses for not.*
  What do parents get for signing?
  If they finance the contract, will you share weekly or monthly results with them?
- *Say when earnings (points) may be cashed in.* Will you exchange points for dollars daily, weekly, monthly, or at the end of the contract?
- *Use strong positives.* Be careful when using food as a positive and when using other positives so important to you that failing to earn them or forfeiting them wreaks havoc in your life.
- *Say how to bring about change.* Will you attempt to rearrange your environment, think more constructively, bring in or take away positives?
- *State direction of change sought.* You want to decrease urges to eat unplanned foods, to increase constructive self-talk, to increase walking.

- *State how context of behavior affects earnings.* Does the 20-minute walk have to be done with family to earn positives?
- *State changes opposed.* You do not want daily calorie intake to be too low. What's too low? Check with your physician or a dietitian. You don't want to skip meals, to fast, or to purge.
- *Redo the contract when necessary.* After a few weeks of no behavior change, reconsider changes sought and ways to obtain them. Do not expect miracles.
- *Avoid narrow and elaborate contracts.* Avoid contracts that address only losing weight or inches and avoid those that target so many actions you weary before you start.
- *Say what and who fuels the contract.* If new clothes back up points earned, who buys the clothes?
- *Say what ends the contract.* Will the contract run until a particular date, until an amount is lost, until named behaviors change, or until some combination of these events happen?

When contract-building, go slowly. Ask what needs changing and who and what will help you make the changes.

ASSERTING YOURSELF

Desperate to be thinner, you ignore that there is no magic-carpet ride to get there. You succumb to the fantasy promises of a new weight-loss craze that demands that you drink daily their "secret" potion and that you pay $150 for a month's supply of the elixir. On arriving home, you belatedly read the fine print about the product. Everything, so promises the brochure, works if you exercise regularly and keep to 1500 calories a day. Realizing that this activity-diet regimen would alone, if followed, thin most adults, at least temporarily (though for many teens the intake would be too low), you suspect the nostrum adds nothing; besides, you learn it contains only water, sugar, fruit juice, two herbs, and two preservatives. What do you do?

You have three options. Option one: Keep the stuff. You think, *It's a long way back to the mall where I bought it, and the saleslady looked as if she could turn nasty. I don't want to hear her whine, "We don't take back Formula K, ever. That's against policy."* But you are out $150 for something worthless.

Option two: Return to the place of purchase, let your anger have sway, and beat the saleslady at her own game of, what you think will be, intimidation. Standing so close to her that she would know the spices in your lunch two hours ago, you could, in your most obnoxious nasal tone, gripe:

> You cheat. This stuff is junk. Listen, I want my money or I'll call the cops.

Option three: Return to the seller and be forthright, clear, and polite, not aggressive. Standing several feet from her, so that neither of you crowds and clouds the other, you could look directly at her and in a modulated, calm voice explain:

> Remember me. I just bought 30 days of your weight-loss drink, but I think I should wait until I'm older. You have been very helpful explaining things to me.

But I'd like my money back. If I decide later I want to try things, I'll come back. Thanks for your help.

Option one is passive: You create no ripples but drown in your own timidity. Option two is aggressive: You create a storm and perhaps drown in a flood of retribution from putting the salesperson on the defensive, a place none wants to be. Option three is assertive: You stand the best chance of getting what you want. No one drowns. Everyone swims. The salesperson is not put off, and because she wants your eventual business likely will do her utmost to satisfy you. Say Drs. Robert Alberti and Michael Emmons, being assertive is standing up for your rights.[5]

"No" is a small word that for many is a hard word. But sometimes it is the only word that will stop friends, parents, grandparents, brothers, and sisters from repeatedly offering you high-fat food and reasons not to exercise. Say no assertively (Chapter 8), not aggressively.

Assert yourself:

- *Rehearse saying no.* Think how you will say no; perhaps, watch yourself in a mirror.
- *Choose words and tone that do not alienate.*
- *Look directly at the person you address.*
- *Speak clearly, calmly, friendly.*
- *Praise your successes.* Perhaps award yourself a positive.

Four methods (thinking better, rearranging the environment, making contracts, and asserting yourself) have now been added to your expanding arsenal of rational overweight control tactics. There is yet more to add, as Chapter 8 illustrates.

CHAPTER 8

TEENS IN CHARGE ————

PLANNING

Know yourself to change yourself. And to know yourself, investigate yourself. This chapter tells you how to investigate, how to be a detective who solves two mysteries—one about eating, one about activity. The method of detection is planning.

Suppose this morning you decide to have an apple for today's after-school snack. It is now afternoon and intensely hot; you could fry an egg on the sidewalk. So on coming home, you are thirsty, not at all hungry. Opening the refrigerator and seeing a half full (32 ounce) bottle of soda, you gulp its irresistible sugar-filled contents. Then, in the mood to eat, you find two slices of apple pie to bolt down. Vaguely remembering something about apple, you push aside the memory until finishing.

You violated the plan to have the apple. How this could happen is the subject of this chapter. To solve the mystery why you do what you do—that is, eat what you eat and drink what you drink and play what you play—lay out intentions, record performances, and find disagreements between these aims and acts.

THE BLUEPRINT OF WHAT TO EAT

To draw up a blueprint of eating, write intentions hours before eating; meals comprise one or more foods.

You are 15 and want to be thinner. Daily calories are to be 250 a day fewer than is typical for you. (Instead of calories, you could, as Drs. John Foreyt and Ken Goodrick show, focus on grams of fat.[1]) Figure 5.1, say, indicates that on average you take in about 2250 calories every 24 hours; so, the new level becomes 2000 calories, a level not markedly lower than RDA guidelines (see Table 2.1). Thinking of the family's typical foods, you and your mother take an hour in the evening to arrange tomorrow's menu.

Table 8.1 is a blueprint of that food plan. On it, you list the foods to be eaten during the morning, afternoon, and evening, noting their quantity and calories. At the top, you set the daily calorie goal at 2000 and write above it Thursday, April 20. At the bottom, you total calories and show a 4-calorie undercut of the 2000-calorie goal. (Seldom will you meet the exact calorie figure; a few less is no problem, but do not regularly undercut by more than 20 or 30.)

On this blueprint of intentions there is another entry added to the total, a 280 calorie entry—the calorie slush fund. Previously, you learned that inflexibility and rigidity spell trouble. Proclaiming french fries, cake, and doughnuts out of your life sets up problems, for breaking "never again commandments" makes you feel incompetent and want to end overweight control.

Skillfully and carefully, Alex Mardsen, a 16-year-old I once treated, would lay out his food intentions the morning of the day planned. A computer devotee, Alex programmed his machine to give details of his favorite dishes—calories, grams of fat, quantity, preparation.

TABLE 8.1. Food Intentions

Day & date: Thursday, April 20
Calorie goal: 2000

	Quantity	Calories[a]	Preparation
Morning meal			
Corn Flakes	3 oz	330	From box
Banana	1 cup		
	(sliced)	125	Raw
Milk	1 glass	102	1%
Afternoon meal			
Whole			
wheat bread	2 slices	110	From package
Bologna (beef)	2 slices	176	From package
Mustard	2 tsp	8	From jar
Orange	1 (med)	71	Raw
Milk	1 glass	102	1%
Evening Meal			
Chicken			
(white, w/o			
skin)	7 oz	330	Roasted
Coleslaw			
(with mayo.)	1 cup	173	Fresh
Milk	1 glass	102	1%
Snacks			
Apple	1 (med)	87	Raw
Calorie slush fund		280	
	Total	1996	

[a]Calories are approximates. Sources for the calorie information are: Watt, B.K., and Merrill, A.L. *Composition of Foods* (Agriculture Handbook No. 8, U.S. Department of Agriculture). Washington, DC: U.S. Government Printing Office; Pennington, J.A.T., and Nichols Church, H. (1980). *Food Values of Portions Commonly Used* (13th ed.). New York: Harper & Row.

Eager and motivated, Alex worked to control his eating, so when he quit treatment I was surprised. His reason for ending it stemmed from breaking two of several "never again commandments." Damning himself as weak and feeling deflated because he broke them, he lost all motivation to continue and, thinking his behavior out of control, stepped closer to future food abuse.

Because he refused to have a slush fund, allowed no room to err, he reacted to the backslide as if it were more than it was. Had he sanctioned having unplanned calories, he might have felt differently about his minor slips. The slush fund says you do not need to plan perfectly. There will be unforeseen extras. Expect them, enjoy them. The slush fund covers most of them. Even if you overdraw the fund, there are ways, explained later, to approach that problem. Don't quit. Don't mock yourself.

Some Tips for Designing the Blueprint

To simplify laying out intentions, store the particulars of favorite dishes (e.g., grams of fat, calories, and so forth) on cards or in a personal computer. Keep calories and fat close to the amount allotted. Ask parents to help arrange menus; much of what you eat, they buy and prepare.

When forecasting snacks and meals, distribute calories as evenly as possible throughout the day: Do not skip breakfast or lunch to have a large dinner, a fattening pattern that trades morning and afternoon starving for evening stuffing. Spreading the allotment over the day means, depending on preferences, having three to six daily meals.

Make the day's blueprint the night before; if doing that is awkward, plan during the morning of the day. Far more important when choosing foods, do not let the words "low cal" fool you. Usually costly and sometimes tasteless, such foods, found in the "diet food" part of the supermarket, may have fewer calories not because of what they contain but because of what they do not—much of the product. Read labels. Buy foods with less fat, not just with few calories. Instead of "low-cal" foods, often pseudobargains, pick regular foods that are genuine bargains, nutritious for the calories they yield.

THE RECORD OF WHAT'S EATEN

Intentions guide, not force, actions. What you promise to do only points you in the right direction. For breakfast, you aim for cereal with milk and fruit, but Dad, without malice, destroys those intentions. He arises early, and because he loves to cook, you awaken to the aromas of bacon frying, pancakes bubbling, and maple syrup warming. There goes your plan.

How closely do you follow your blueprint? Table 8.2, the meal record, lets you answer. Listing the same characteristics of food as does Table 8.1 (type, quantity, calories, and preparation), it tells about one meal:

- What meal it is—B for breakfast (morning meal), L for lunch (afternoon meal), D for dinner (evening meal), and S for snack
- What number meal it is (the number of meals before it plus 1)
- When you begin it
- How you feel before beginning it (hungry, happy, sad, bored, lonely, angry, frightened)
- How many calories in it
- How many calories (last line) have been used so far during the day

TABLE 8.2. Sample Meal Record

Day & date of record: Friday, April 21

Meal: B ⓛ D S   Meal no. today = 2

		Quantity	Calories	Preparation
Food 1	Whole wheat bread	2 slices	110	From package
Food 2	Bologna (beef)	2 slices	176	From package
Food 3	Mustard	2 tsp	8	From jar
Food 4	Orange	1 (med)	71	Raw
Food 5	Milk	1 glass	102	1%
Food 6				
Food 7				
Food 8				

Total calories for meal = 467

Time begin eating = 1:30

Feeling before eating = bored

Total calories thus far today = 1024

Table 8.2 shows that it is lunch, the second meal of the day. It begins at 1:30 P.M. with the recorder being bored. Total calories for the meal equals 467 and total to that point in the day equals 1024. Particularly helpful, this last entry informs you meal by meal about calories—what's gone, what's left. Table 8.3, the record of the evening meal, shows that total calories for the day, which includes breakfast, lunch, snack, and dinner, is now 1716. What remains is the 280-calorie slush fund.

TABLE 8.3. Sample Meal Record
Day & date of record: Friday, April 21
Meal: B L Ⓓ S   Meal no. today = 4

	Quantity	Calories	Preparation
Food 1 Chicken (white, w/o skin)	7 oz	330	Roasted
Food 2 Coleslaw (with mayo.)	1 cup	173	Fresh
Food 3 Milk	1 glass	102	1%
Food 4			
Food 5			
Food 6			
Food 7			
Food 8			

Total calories for meal = 605

Time begin eating = 6:30

Feeling before eating = hungry

Total calories thus far today = 1716

WHY FOOD PLANS FALL APART

What rips the blueprint? To find out, pivotal to the planning approach, the detective compares intentions with actions, compares blueprint with meal record, and if they disagree, thinks about why they disagree. When you know the plan-breakers and how and when they strike, you move closer to forecasting and controlling them; understanding precedes predicting and predicting precedes controlling.

One food plan-breaker or several arising together can demolish good intentions. For clarity, I illustrate food plan-breakers separately, but combinations are typical and others, not here listed, possible.

Food plan-breakers cause extra eating. Worse, they cause teens to misinterpret unwanted eating as signs of helplessness, hopelessness, and worthlessness, misconceptions that provoke dangerous dieting (Chapter 3).

Food on My Mind

You spend an hour on Tuesday evening forecasting Wednesday's meals. It is now Wednesday 11:00 A.M., History class is in full swing, and you are bored. As the teacher drones on about the Battle of Hastings and 1066 A.D., you focus not on the color, barbarism, and gore of battle but on chocolates.

Whenever bored or sad or stressed, you want something sweet, especially something chocolate. Walking home to have your well-planned lunch, you detour to the drugstore and buy two chocolate bars, large bars, to enjoy on the trip.

Food Probably There

Food is everywhere. You do not have to see it to know it is close by or to want it. If your home stocks almost as many foods as a small market does, if you need no map to find the rich, fatty treasures that abide therein, and if your intentions are vague, you will likely eat more than you want to.

It's summer. Sixteen-year-old Malcolm Johannsen finishes his afternoon deliveries early, goes home, and turns on the television. Hungry, he wants to snack but hasn't forecasted what to have. Nothing written leaves him unprotected, letting his immediate wants fuel his active imagination and guide his subsequent action. He knows that the freezer has three quarts of extra-rich vanilla ice cream, the lazy Susan tray holds an opened tin of butter-scotch sauce, and the cupboard houses cashews and mara-schino cherries. Putting information together, he turns fantasy into reality and, despite his desire to be thinner, enjoys a rich sundae.

Food Clearly There

You try to eat fewer fatty foods to slim down. Seventeen days of Christmas vacation begin tomorrow, and your three best friends invite you to join them at the fast-food place across from school. You agree to, reluctantly. Planning to have a diet drink, that is all you plan; you know the restaurant stocks delicious foods.

Yet there is something else about the place that affects your eating. Smell. As you enter, you smell french fries frying; the aroma of crisping potatoes overpowers you. After requesting the diet drink, your nose compels you to order the fries. The smell of tasty food is for many a food plan-breaker.

Still more of a goad to eating is the sight of tasty food, party food—chips and dip, bacon-wrapped morsels, tiny spicy meatballs on toothpicks. The table displaying them invites sampling, and that sampling happens regardless of whether you are angry, bored, sad, or hungry. Seeing tasty food is an inescapable, forcible cue to eat it.

Food to Celebrate

Besides knowledge, smell, and sight, your eating at the fast-food restaurant falls under the spell of another food

plan-breaker: celebration. You eat to mark an occasion—
here, the start of Christmas vacation.

Will we ever exercise instead of eat to make merry?
Our culture says use food to celebrate; food is the time-
honored tribute. Few of us would go for a jog to mark the
arrival of our favorite aunt or a stroll by the river to
applaud an "A" in Biology. We have wedding breakfasts,
not wedding walks, and take famous people to dinner, not
to the gym. We punctuate good times—the holidays, the
visits of relatives, the triumphs of friends, our dates, our
achievements—with food.

Seeing Others Eat

There is another impulse to eat at the fast-food restaurant,
another food plan-breaker. On entering the place, you not
only smell and see food, but also see and hear others
enjoying it—talking, laughing, chomping, munching. It is
difficult not to eat when everyone around you eats. Seeing
and hearing others enjoy food, whether you like or dislike
or feel neutral toward them, compels you to try to do as
they do. You find it almost impossible to sit with nothing
to eat, especially when others eating sit at your table.

Food Heroics

Despite the food plan-breakers challenging you at the
fast-food place, you have only the planned diet drink, and
so feel powerful and in control. As well, when leaving, you
feel deprived and deserving. Arriving home, knowing Dad
has baked shortbread cookies and other delights of the
season, and feeling meritorious for successfully jumping
the hurdles of the fast-food restaurant, you reward yourself with 18 cookies.

Food Friends

Once I treated an overweight woman who complained of a food friend in her family, her mother. Of Ukrainian descent, my patient, who lived alone, loved the pierogies (small rectangular potato-filled or cheese-filled delicacies) and holubchi (cabbage roles stuffed with meat) her mother prepared. Weekly dinners at mother's were a prelude to her problem: receiving an elaborate, well-stocked, arranged-with-love, irresistible, take-home basket.

Unwittingly, mother (preparer of the food basket) turned kindness into cruelty. Because my patient struggled to control her intake and because early in the morning she would devour everything in the take-home basket, she would repeatedly berate herself, "I've no self-respect, I'm weak."

My patient's parent was her food friend. Your parents may be your food friends, concocting rich treats or buying them and being insulted if you do not enjoy them. By their behavior, they say I slave for you and this is how you treat me.

Friends may inadvertently become food friends, tempting and frustrating you with their gifts. Food pushers,not evildoers, they subtly let you know that to decline what they offer is somehow, someway, to rebuff them.

Time to Burn

You drive downtown one morning to take advantage of a sale at a sporting-goods store. The sale is a yearly event, and to get values you arrive early—40 minutes before the store opens. Growing restless after 20 minutes, you walk to a nearby market to buy two sweetrolls. Experience has taught you that having time to burn creates a vacuum that food fills. Eating makes waiting tolerable, and therefore having time to burn and food nearby creates ideal conditions for breaking food plans.

Clean the Plate

One evening, your mother, father, younger brother, and you dine at an expensive steak house. While ordering a costly meal of onion soup, Caesar salad, filet mignon, baked potato, and green beans in hollandaise sauce, you hear Dad's quiet "Ahem"—his throaty sound when he has to pay high prices. Thirty minutes after dinner comes, five forkfuls of the expensive beef remain on your plate. Full but daring not leave a morsel, you stuff what's left.

Laying down knife and fork before the meat disappears risks scorn for being wasteful. From your earliest days, your parents and theirs have reminded, "There are starving children who would gladly take your place at the dinner table." To want not, waste not.

Clean your plate. Years ago, you were paid off with dessert for following this edict. Now, though unable to hold another bite, even if it were a creamy, cheesy, flaky bite, you are distressed if part of the entree remains.

Food is expensive, and there are hungry people everywhere who would love your good fortune. But eating unwanted food does nothing to solve these problems. Better would be to take less. Better would be not to force finishing. Better, when without control over quantity served, would be to share the bounty with others at the table.

Food Comforts Me

In Chapter 6, we mentioned some of the work of the famous psychiatrist Dr. Hilde Bruch, who argued that for many of us eating ties up with emotions.[2] If when we were small, our parents, grandparents, aunts, and uncles repeatedly gave us candy, cakes, cookies, and ice cream to quell our anger, to relieve our sadness, to remove our boredom, and to heighten our joy, we will now bind food to those feelings. We will now eat to ease unpleasant emotions and amplify pleasant ones.

Sometimes if feeling turmoil, lonely, rejected, or alienated, or if downtrodden because pants squeeze and stomach protrudes, you will turn to food for comfort. For awhile, it will comfort.

But not without cost: feeling bad for having eaten, eating still more, and soon feeling worse. You tumble into the destructive downward spiral of eating, regretting eating, feeling terrible, eating more, and regretting more. Those aching for quick loss and willing to suffer restrictive, punishing, unhealthy diets know well the spiral.

WHAT TO DO WHEN PLANS COLLAPSE

To erase the impact of a food plan-breaker, estimate its cost—its extra calories, its fat grams—and replan. So if the problem has been "food clearly there" and you have consumed a few hundred extra calories beyond the slush fund, increase subsequent exercise. For the next several days, upgrade daily activity from an hour of basketball, volleyball, or badminton to two hours of one of them; there are many ways to overcome the setback, partly or totally.

Or, do nothing. If not repeatedly slipping, accept the slip. You need not make up for it. Say to yourself:

> *Okay, I had the fries, so what. I enjoyed them. I'm not going to blow up like a balloon because of them. I'm going to*

renew my efforts to eat better. And I'm not going to cut my
calories to a starvation level. I'll be rational, not irrational.
I'll help myself, not hurt myself.

Work to limit unwanted calories and unwanted grams of fat. Work to stop self-blame and the unhealthy practices it spawns. Recouping is trying to recover from the physical and psychological impacts of food plan-breakers.

To prevent a food plan-breaker from happening again, reflect. Think about and apply tactics this book espouses—bringing in positives, contracting, rearranging your world, asserting yourself, and so on. So, to stop the repeat of the "food on my mind" plan-breaker involving candy, contract to resist chocolate-eating urges. Award points backed up by positives for defying cravings. Because feeling bored, sad, or stressed probably sets up wanting chocolates, target these feelings in the contract and, if the situation permits, do something enjoyable or relaxing when they arise. Give points for whatever you do that blocks the urge.

To govern the "food probably there" plan-breaker, plan better. Malcolm Johannsen, described earlier in this chapter, could have rearranged his world so that he had better snacks ready. Likewise, to control the "food clearly there," "food to celebrate," "seeing others eat," and "food heroics" plan-breakers, plan better. Award positives. Take away positives. Rearrange your world. Design contracts. Think constructively.

Arm yourself to control overweight. Tell parents un-eaten food on your plate is waste to throw out, not to consume; is garbage to discard, not to digest. Tell food friends you want not their food but their friendship. To interrupt the downward spiral "food as comfort" causes, tell yourself you rule your food world. To fill the vacuum "time to burn" creates, list activities to do in lieu of eating.

Reflect on preventing plan-breakers. And take heed: What works for you may not for someone else, and what works for you today may not in a year, a month, or a week.

PLANNING AND EXERCISE

Judging from the numbers of teenagers who diet, you must agree that many if not most teens would rather eat less than move more, would rather fast than walk a few extra miles or play a few extra hours of sports. But rational, healthful overweight control requires rational, healthful exercise.

For the sake of your body, your emotions, your outlook, live the active life. Because overweight and inactivity often share the same body, we (at our clinic) try to help teenagers understand why activity beats inactivity. We want them to see the pluses of sports, walks, and active recreation, to enjoy moving more, and to carry forward this pleasure into adulthood. The method of planning applies to exercise: laying out exercise intentions, recording exercises, finding exercise-breakers, recouping, and reflecting.

But before employing it, know those beliefs interfering with your becoming and staying active.

BELIEFS PROMOTING INACTIVITY

One, exercise hard to thin down. Deceptive. Leave home and run, walk, or swim enough to lose a pound of fat, and you will return exhausted, maybe ill. To burn 3500 calories, on average the calories in a pound of fat, requires traveling miles and miles. To exercise that much without suffering, to drop a pound of fat in one flurry of maniacal activity without injury, requires great stamina and conditioning.

Do not let the hard-exercise, hard-body belief rule. Exercise pays off for the overweight and taxes them less when done gradually: Do small, manageable amounts of it daily—not intense, not depleting, not overwhelming. Walk, swim, bike, or run, but leave marathons for the future or for the marathoner.

Another belief promoting inactivity, one conceived in narrow thinking, is that losing pounds is what's important, all that's important; the scale becomes *the* barometer. But scales, as mentioned, can be unreliable. What's more, losing pounds is not the only or best goal; losing fat is better. To make the fat part of each lost pound sizable, exercise. Pursue the active life.

Yet another activity-paralyzing belief is that exercise causes hunger. True, but again deceptive. Walk fast around the neighborhood in fall and you might increase appetite. But those who would rather sit than stand, the sedentary, often eat more than do those who would just stroll around the neighborhood, do light calisthenics, or swim briefly. Not always does a moderate amount of activity stimulate the appetite. In fact, indicated nutritionist Dr. Jean Mayer long ago, exercise may diminish it.[3]

Therapists at our clinic uncover beliefs that deactivate teenagers and try to foster those that activate them. Here's a sample of what our patients read:

> We act as if spending energy were stupid and wasteful. We hate to move. And we don't hide this hatred. We buy telephone extensions to prevent miles of

walking, drive everywhere rather than walk anywhere, have remote controls on our stereos to save
steps, have our younger brothers and sisters fetch and
carry for us, watch hours of TV each day, rent videos,
go to movies, play boardgames. If possible, we'd buy
a robot to do our chores.

But deactivating dams up energy. The less we
move, the less we want to move, and the less fit and
more overweight we remain. Stop inactivity. Ride
less, move more: stand up, walk, run, and play.

To know if you move more, to know if you eat better,
keep records (Chapter 5).

BLOCKS TO MOVING MORE

Thoughts, self-talk, and actions can interfere with improving not only eating but also exercising, creating blocks to
becoming more active. I'll present those barriers we commonly see; combinations and other obstacles are, of course,
possible.

Embarrassment

Tall and 40 pounds overweight, you decide to play intra-
mural sports. Signing up for the basketball team, attending
a practice session, and working up a good sweat, you then
quit, imagining that others laugh at your exercising in
T-shirt and shorts. Jumping, running, stretching are not for
the overweight, so you think.

Numbers of teenagers, many themselves overweight,
consider the heavy fast-walking, slow-jogging, tennis-
playing boy or girl comical and so avoid activity; they fear

ridicule. Better, they feel, to hide in front of the TV than to exercise in front of others, especially in front of friends and classmates. Like Michael (Chapter 1), they want to be permanently excused from gym.

Society's attack on the overweight underlies their embarrassment. But, as discussed, the assault is misguided and groundless.

It must not keep you from the active life. Do not let shame tie knots and restrict opportunity. Regardless of what others say or think, move more and likely soon you will want to move more.

Overdoing

Sixteen and somewhat heavy, you want to diet but the doctor says, "Just walk more." She knows you do the minimum in gym and hate sports, enjoying instead Monopoly, checkers, chess, TV soaps, and movies.

But though shunning exercise, you want to be trimmer. So one day, feeling vigorous, you flex your muscles, breathe deeply, and propose during the coming week to swim 40 minutes three times and run six miles seven times. Using the format of Figure 5.3 to write intentions and actions, you meet goals on day 1 but quit on day 2. By planning too much, you do too little. Your diary records, "It wiped me out, it took up my whole Saturday. Besides, today I'm too sore. There has to be an easier way." There is.

Boredom

You are not embarrassed to exercise. And your hating it means there is no danger of your overdoing it. Here, the block to the plan is your finding exercise dull. You would almost rather get a cavity filled than ride a stationary bike indoors on a warm summer evening, jog the same six blocks day after day, swim laps until waterlogged, or walk around the same park for the 100th time. But exercise need not bore.

Stuck

You plan 30-minute walks for Monday through Friday mornings before school. That coupled with cutting back on doughnuts during the day and chips and dip during the evening in front of the television will, you believe, help you look better on the beach this summer.

Today it is freezing, but that does not faze you. It is complying with father's request that you drive your brother to school that dissolves plans. Ordinarily, little brother takes the city bus, but for the past few days he has been bedridden with the flu and, although feeling better, is still prey for the February wind.

You would like to refuse Dad but cannot, having just won over him and your mother by arguing that their helping you finance a new-model used car would add to not only your pleasure but also their freedom; another car and driver in the family would ease their transportation burden.

Two days later, you again foul the exercise plan: It is pouring outside and walking in water would be awful, let alone foolish.

Driving brother is like the rain in that both have sway over you, blocking intentions to walk in the morning. To handle the unforeseen, to not let family, friends, or Mother Nature demolish good intentions, do not get stuck on one exercise. Have alternative exercises ready.

Busy

You do much: school, homework, meals with the family, maybe a job sitting behind a convenience-store gas station counter three evenings a week taking cash and making change. It may seem that you are too busy to be active, have a schedule so filled with sit-down acts that it seems there is no time to swim, to ski, to roller skate, to snow-shoe, to play volleyball, to walk.

But when exercise becomes a priority, you can be busy and exercise, too.

DOING SOMETHING ABOUT EXERCISE-BREAKERS

As with food plan-breakers, recoup from exercise-breakers and be reasonable when you try to: Just as you are not to starve after stuffing, you are not to exhaust yourself after doing little or nothing. Do not follow a week of idleness with a weekend of herculean labor: Do not swim, jog, and bike miles and miles Saturday if you did no more than study, write papers, and listen to teachers Monday through Friday. If basketball planned for Monday is not played, recoup Tuesday; play it or something like it on that day; if not Tuesday, pick Wednesday, and so on.

Besides recouping, reflect on removing the blocks to moving more: Think better, rearrange your world, contract with yourself. For instance, you want to walk two miles to the park every day after school, but the first day, 100 yards outside of your front door, you turn back. Your stomach hosts a Ping-Pong tournament, and something hot and prickly crawls on your face—you are embarrassed.

Try to think differently and contract with yourself to gradually increase the distance. Ask what's embarrassing about walking two miles to the park. What's going on in your head that makes you worry? Perhaps, feeling grotesque and burlesque, you think:

> *If somebody sees me, they'll laugh and tell everyone how funny I look. I'll be laughed at. That's worse than dying.*

Challenge these negative thoughts:

> *I don't want to be seen, but if I am so what? So what if some jerk laughs? I'm not responsible for what fools do. I have to do what's good for me. I doubt anyone will be that interested in my exercising to spread the news. Who would care to know? Even if someone is pathetic enough to want to spread it, I won't die. It's important that I do what's good for me, that I do what I want to.*

Read over the challenges. Then, dressing comfortably, go about a half mile and return home. Two days later, feeling more confident, go again but add about a quarter mile to the previous success, more if possible. Keep adding distance every few days; add when comfortable enough to add—when the panic over being seen is manageable. The contract awards points for going farther and farther—more points for more distance. Designate how many points buys what—10, a movie; 40, a new jacket; 60, a new camera. Better self-talk and the contract will help attain goals. You will prize progress, the conquest of shame.

To handle problems of too much exercise, boredom, being stuck, and too busy, lay out intentions that, on reflection, do not intrude greatly on your free time. Get to know activities: dancing, tennis, racquetball, basketball, squash, rope jumping, soccer, handball, cross-country skiing, downhill skiing, snowshoeing, roller skating, ice skating, Ping-Pong, and more. They vary in not only how much they require of you but also how comfortably they fit into your day.

Separate activities into three classes: those you hate now and think you always will; those you might come to like; those you do like. Perhaps swimming seems bothersome, badminton has potential, and walking, no special attire or facility required, is acceptable. Select, begin beneath capabilities, and add gradually and progressively to successes. Also, make some activities alternatives for times when the weather, parents, sister or brother, or a friend forces you to abandon plans.

Name the positives to be awarded if plans are followed and those to be removed if plans are not. Rearrange your environment to promote better actions. Assert yourself with others who interfere, and contract with yourself about when to do what.

As well, consider writing a contract with a friend to make exercising more fun. Negotiate the exercise to do, when to do it, and consequences to you and your partner for doing and for not doing it. Suppose your parents agree to allow you to take a train with your best friend 100 miles to a resort; your friend gets the same okay from her parents. Both of you want to slim some before the trip and decide to exercise. After discussing options, the two of you recognize that more tennis, a game each of you enjoys, will help.

Scheduled hour-long tennis matches are to earn points toward the combined price of the two tickets for the trip; 500 points entitles the purchase. Each completed session of exercise nets each of you 5 points. So, if all goes well, after 50 matches each of you has 250 points and the right to purchase tickets, the price of which you evenly split.

Suppose also if one of you misses a scheduled match, she loses out on getting the 5 points but the other person still gets hers. Breaking an appointment costs. Not living up to promises, not exercising as planned, delays the trip because it takes longer to accumulate the 500 points.

Further, let's agree, not keeping the contracted-for promises means paying more of the trip: She who fails to follow the contract pays more of the combined price of two tickets. Make the percent of the total number of points one earns toward the trip the percent of the total cost the other pays. Because of misses, there are eventually 60 instead of 50 scheduled matches. You show up for all of them; your partner comes to 40. You earn 300 (60 × 5) points—60% of the trip; your partner, 200 points—40% of the trip. Fractions forgotten, but infractions not, she pays 60% of the cost of the two tickets, and you pay only 40%.

However you handle exercise-breakers, closely watch what happens. Sometimes by itself recording frees you from repeating problems. As applied to eating and exercising, the planning method says:

- *Lay out intentions.* Remember, apropos of planning foods, do not box yourself in. Have a slush fund.
- *Record performances.*
- *Compare aims and actions and pinpoint the reasons that cause them to disagree.* I have named ten food plan-breakers and five exercise-breakers. Others are possible and combinations likely.
- *Recoup.* Increase exercise.

- *Reflect.* Using principles and tactics for changing behavior, try to prevent problems from recurring.

In this and the two preceding chapters, we have focused on ways to eat more sensibly and to exercise more frequently. In Chapter 9, we describe difficulties that prevent such methods from working.

CHAPTER **9**

PROBLEMS GETTING AND STAYING WHERE YOU WANT —

Slimming is not simple. Many teenagers who try to become less overweight do not. Why they do not remains a mystery. For some, perhaps, it is the faulty regimens they try: restrictive diets, fad diets, herculean exercise, or combinations thereof. But even the best programs fail.

Still less understood is why many teens who do reach their goals cannot hold onto their achievements.

To help you change shape and overweight, I have in this book emphasized the slow, the rational, the liberal. Experience and experiments allow me to emphasize that.

To help you keep the changes made, I have less to draw from. My main sources of information are what I have done to myself and for the overweight teenagers I see in my practice. Few experiments study the healthy things teenagers do to stay thinner.

PROBLEMS GETTING WHERE YOU WANT TO BE

I name seven problems. Likely there are others, and those I identify sometimes combine to make slimming extremely difficult.

Feeling Pressured to Lose

Rearranging your world, contracting, planning, and so on, you start to stop being overweight. Prospects for thinning look good. But after a week or two of listening to internal dialogues, challenging destructive thoughts, eating better, and moving more, you quit.

You never wanted to start overweight control in the first place. Perhaps friends, brothers and sisters, or parents said that you would be good-looking if only you were thin or, attempting to shame, implied or said that thin is in and fat is ugly.

Being different from the pack is okay. As author Elaine Landau endorses in her book, *Weight: A Teenage Concern*, involve yourself not with being different, but with making a difference.[1] Wait until you want to control overweight. That may not happen for awhile, maybe never will.

Everyone Knows

Fat at 16, I was, according to my doctor, who happened to be my grandfather, about 60 pounds overweight. Tired of the epithets my peers threw at me, I dieted and exercised. And I lost 40 pounds. To celebrate this and my graduating from high school, I traveled from my Los Angeles home to Montreal during the second summer of my program. Soon after arriving, I quit the program.

I had stopped and started before, but this time I ended the regimen less because I hated it and more because my best friend wouldn't be quiet about it. Proud of my successes, he had boasted that I had that powerful, sought-after, mystical, magical internal strength he fondly, reverently, and authoritatively called "willpower." By broadcasting my weight loss, he embarrassed me. Never will I forget his relatives' smiles when they heard of my overweight control triumphs or their questions about how I, a young man, could resist what they, older and fatter and wiser, could not. I felt so visible. To stop the feeling, I stopped the program.

Today, I do not care who knows I watch what I eat and monitor my exercise, but at that time in my life I cared deeply. Perhaps you feel now as I felt then. Rather than quit if your secret gets out, ask why the revelation bothers you. Challenge what you find.

Hating the Program

Under no pressure to, you try to control overweight. Weeks later, though, hating all the do's and don'ts, you quit trying. Possibly, at the start you ate at specific times, in specific places, with specific plates, glasses, and silverware. As well, you planned menus, recorded consumption, searched for food plan-breakers, and followed an exhausting exercise schedule. Possibly, in addition, you tracked and revamped thoughts and adhered to detailed contracts that awarded and removed positives. You threw everything into your program all at once and now, overburdened, throw it all away.

Perhaps kinder, you nonetheless deprived yourself: removed all ready-to-eat snack foods from home, ceased watching television during the school week, swore to no more birthday cake, launched a no-dessert policy. After several weeks, missing what's gone and angry about what's left (overweight), you quit. The program robbed more than it enriched.

Or, although gradual about instituting methods and generous about limits, perhaps you stopped the program because some tactics seemed stupid:

It makes no difference if I eat only with a designated spoon, knife, and fork. It makes no difference if I eat only at designated times.

Doubting the worth of some tactics, you stopped all tactics: every rearrangement, every challenge to destructive thinking, every clause of the negotiated contract. In the wake of hatred for part of the program, you obliterated the entire program.

And, from doing too much, depriving too much, and discarding too much, your motivation flew away.

Avoid feeling overburdened: Add a method only when comfortable with those already there. Counter feeling deprived: Return some of the pleasures erased; do not suddenly, sweepingly forbid all TV and all desserts, prohibit all birthday cake, banish all snack foods. Be gradual, not abrupt; be flexible, not rigid; cut down, not out.

Curtail those elements of the program you perceive, after trying them, to be useless. If avoiding the bakery seems after awhile to be off target, eliminate that procedure. If asserting yourself with a food friend causes dissension more than it avoids grams of fat, stop the assertion. If going to after-school volleyball aggravates more than trims, find another exercise.

Feeling That the Program Isn't Working

You think, *Weeks of effort and not much lighter.* Maybe the program has failed, maybe it has not. As said, weight loss tells only one thing about it, and not the best thing about it: Weight loss is not the only goal, weight loss is a delayed outcome of other changes, weight loss is not identical to fat loss. Before concluding that the program has failed, see if clothes fit better, see if you feel better, see if you move more and eat better.

Feeling Outside

Every Christmas, I watch at least one version of the Dickens classic, *A Christmas Carol.* Its star, the cantankerous old miser Scrooge, lives on warmed-over gruel.

Numbers of teenagers trying to be less overweight believe that their diets are as dull as Scrooge's, especially when they contrast their fare with that of their brothers, sisters, and parents. Even if eating sensibly, the watchful teenager may still feel cheated and alone, as if a castout in his own home.

Demanding, cajoling, and getting everyone in the family to give up what he gives up rids him of the outsider feeling, but invites the label "troublemaker." Other family members rail at their losses as a result of what they perceive as his selfishness: "It's your problem, not ours. Why should we suffer?"

No matter if you go it alone or if brothers, sisters, and parents agree to eat what you eat, change the diet gradually only. Slow, step-by-step change increases the palatability of the new bill of fare.

Better still, escape comparisons that identify you as outcast or troublemaker: Rely more on exercise and emphasize burning calories, not limiting calories.

Feeling Rejected

Doing your best to control overweight, you still hear, "Hey fat ass, you're a pig." Detractors still roam school halls.

And their insults still hurt. On hearing them, perhaps you want to escape through television and eat something sweet and rich.

When others are nasty and you want to end over-weight control, listen to your thoughts:

> *No matter how hard I try, I'm always the butt of their jokes. Why bother? It's no use.*

If well and unconcerned about overweight control, you have an argument for not attempting change. But if you want to battle overweight, challenge the "it's no use" thought:

> *I bother to do what I'm doing because I want to. It's for me, no one else. I'm going about it carefully and realistically, and even if others are mean, I won't stop something I want to do.*

Feeling Unsupported

Your parents, like Michael's of Chapter 1, love you. Sometimes they show this affection in ways you wish they did not: They bake spaghetti with heaps rather than sprinkles of cheese, they concoct cherry turnovers with twice the butter and twice the syrupy cherries called for, they double the chocolate on your favorite cookies. Far from rejecting, they are caring.

But their style of caring makes you feel misunderstood, downplayed, unsupported. You think, *How can I follow a program here? I'm killed with kindness.* Tell them. Be assertive. If eating Dad's fancy breakfast would demolish not only the slush fund (Chapter 8) but also your zest to continue the program, tell him this:

> *Thanks, but I need to stick to my plan. What you made really smells great, but I have to say no this time. Please understand.*

PROBLEMS STAYING WHERE YOU WANT TO STAY

After months of planning, deciding, recording, sweating, many of you will be less or no longer overweight and, feeling triumphant, will stop your programs. Some of you who do so will remain thinner and fitter; others will not—will regain overweight, get fatter, lose fitness. Without hardly noticing, some of you will begin to eat as before and start to slide into past sedentary ways. We cannot predict who will and who will not prosper during the long, long period after overweight control. As psychologist Dr. Thomas Wadden of the University of Pennsylvania and his colleagues write:

> Maintenance of weight loss is the Achilles' heel of weight control efforts with adults and appears to be with adolescents as well. (p. 350)[2]

I will give some reasons why staying less overweight is so difficult.

Setpoint

Studies, many of them conducted by University of Wisconsin researcher Dr. Richard Keesey, suggest that the body, like a muscular lineman of a top football team, defends its weight—its customary weight, its setpoint weight.[3] Existing within you, so says the theory, are pressures to keep things constant.

Change is resisted. Gaining forces into action internal pressures to lose. Losing forces into action internal pressures to gain. The body drives those who have lost weight, fallen beneath setpoint, to put the weight back on and those who have gained weight, gone beyond setpoint, to take it off. The setpoint is the weight where any change from it starts this inner pushing—below setpoint the push is to go up, above setpoint the push is to go down.

If winter chills your bones, you rely on a device in your house that relies on setpoint, heat setpoint. Suppose you set it, the household thermostat, at 70 degrees. When brother runs outside on 30 degree days and leaves the front door ajar, your house loses its heat. Because the inside temperature falls below 70 degrees, the furnace comes on. Shut the door, the house warms to setpoint, the heat turns off.

Setpoint theory says there are pressures on weight losers, like there are on cold houses, to return to previous levels, to established setpoints. About the time of World War II, convincing a sample of male volunteers to semi-starve, Dr. Ancel Keys and his colleagues in Minnesota studied the effects of going below setpoint.[4] For awhile, the food-deprived men in the Keys experiment lost weight, but then even though daily calories remained low, they could not continue losing. Their calorie (energy) needs decreased. The body's natural output of energy, energy to breathe, to pump blood—fuel to live (metabolic rate)—dropped. Adjusting to getting fewer calories, the body lowered its requirements. It was as if the body said to itself, "Feed me less, I'll need less"—defended against losing weight.

Similarly, there are strains on weight gainers, though the return to the past takes the opposite path. Years ago, Drs. Eathan Sims and Edward Horton, then in Vermont, fed prisoners, again volunteers, large amounts of food, way more than the men would customarily get in jail.[5] The men gained, but they could not maintain their higher weights; some convicts even had trouble gaining at all.

Do not think of setpoint as something that will forever lock you inside an overweight body. There's no direct proof of that. Also, there's no proof that setpoint stays constant no matter what. Indeed, Dr. Alvin Silverstein and his colleagues declare in their book for teens, *So You Think You're Fat?*, that exercise, if done regularly, can change setpoint.[6]

Thinking Gains Are Relapses

Many of you will get taller. So, many of you will get heavier, but the added pounds do not necessarily mean added fat. When the scale reading goes up, find out if gains are beyond what is expected for your age, sex, and height. Ask your doctor and, if they are, renew efforts; start controlling overweight again. Under no circumstances conclude you are hopeless and helpless.

Snack Attacks

Nearly everyone snacks—some between breakfast and lunch, some between lunch and dinner, some after dinner, some at all of these times. Nothing is wrong with snacking.

The problems lie with the specifics: what the snack is, how much of it there is, how often snacking occurs during the day and evening.

Every now and then, check on the type, quantity, and daily frequency of your snacks and take note if you are snacking more today than you did when you stopped actively controlling overweight; make a food record (e.g., Figure 5.1). See if more snacks now occur with favorite TV shows, if study-time snacks are still vegetables, if snacks after school have changed from apples and oranges to chocolates and cheesecake or from carrots and celery to fudge cookies and strawberry ice cream.

Activities Diminish

During a typical day, 15-year-old David Matthew enjoys six pieces of French toast, three bologna sandwiches (four slices of meat per sandwich), and three bowls of cereal. He washes down all of this, which he consumes besides his three daily gargantuan meals, with a daily half gallon of skim milk. Obesity runs in his family, yet he is not at all fat.

Whether genes protect him against obesity—it would seem in his family they would not—I do not know. What is clear is how much he exercises: walks miles daily, shovels snow throughout the long harsh winter, splits logs for firewood (three-fourths of a cord every seven days), pumps iron hours at a time (several times a week), and practices and plays tackle football six days out of every seven in fall. David has a killer exercise schedule. Recommend it, I don't. But it does suggest that activity controls corpulence, for David eats anything he wants, whenever he wants.

Using the activity forms of this book, watch for the reappearance of barren times in your activity life. Comparing now to the end of the program, check whether you still walk as much, use the car as little, ask brothers and sisters to fetch and carry as rarely, watch television as infrequently. By all means enjoy television, checkers, chess, movies, and videos; inactivity has its place. But enjoy, too, football, racquetball, tennis, and skiing. And keep on enjoying them.

"Never Agains" Come Again

Having worked to overcome overweight, you vow never again to buy doughnuts or turnovers, never again to buy chili dogs and fries, never again to have onion rings, candy bars, soft drinks, cookies, cake, or homemade pie. Likely, you will break these promises, for they are unrealistic. Promises to control treats, not to banish treats, are realistic.

Earlier, I pointed out why not to let "never agains" muddy the overweight control plan and (if you do let them intrude) how the slush fund helps clean up much of the mess. Boxing yourself in with "never agains" occurs after the program, too. Saying goodbye forever to rich foods and later saying hello to them makes you feel downtrodden, guilty, and angry. Broken "never again" promises instigate self-denigration and make too much out of too little.

Embracing the Broken Leg Metaphor

This trap ensnares easily. And generally it contributes to the traps of snacking more, moving less, and making ironclad resolutions, which turn out to be more like silly-putty.

Months have gone by since you started rearranging your world, modifying self-talk, and asserting with food friends. Style of living has changed, overweight has become history. Happy, you stop the program believing the problem solved. It is and it is not.

There have been changes, changes you want, but changes are not irrevocable. Often troubles return. Believing that they will not, that no longer need you be concerned because no longer are you overweight, embraces the broken leg metaphor.

Break a leg, the doctor sets and casts it, and it mends. In time, after maddening itching and ingenious scratching systems (hooray for unbent coat hangers), you heal and return to the life you had before the mishap. Unless again you climb trees or ladders to do handstands in high places to delight those safe below, chances are your legs will stay straight and strong; the mended limb stays mended. Mostly, common sense ensures well-being.

Unlike the leg that knits after the break, the newly thinner body requires a long, long vigil and a constant lookout to keep it thinner. Watch it or it will not stay thinner. Although the person whose leg has healed can in the main forget the injury, the person newly freed of overweight has to stay cautious, far more cautious.

TIPS TO TRY TO STAY THINNER

- Remain vigilant. To track percent overweight, make a graph:
    Draw two lines to form a right angle.
    Label the line on the bottom of the graph

"months" and the line going upwards from it "percent overweight."

Draw another horizontal line above the bottom of the graph—"zero percent overweight."

Keep near this second horizontal line, going neither below nor far above it.

Graph monthly, and post the graph in your room. (Ask your family doctor to help you keep up the graph.)

- Eat sensibly.

    Lessen fats and sugars.

    Rarely stuff, never starve.

    Strive for a balanced diet that includes fruits, vegetables, breads, cereals, meat, fish, poultry, and low-fat or no-fat milk (see Chapter 3).

    Eat foods high in nutrition for the calories they yield.

- Minimize hunger. Try to distribute calories equally throughout the day.

- Maximize activity.

    Keep exercises manageable, comfortable, and enjoyable.

    Walk more.

- Reappraise periodically what, how much, and how often you eat (especially snack).

- Reappraise periodically how much and how often you exercise.

- Watch that "never agains" never again take over.

- Counter destructive thoughts—those making too much of occasional treats—with constructive thoughts.

- Ask for the help of your parents and others when trying to maintain progress.

Up to now, I have talked directly to teenagers. The next chapter addresses parents and those professionals concerned with the health, happiness, and prosperity of young people.

CHAPTER 10

FOR PARENTS AND PROFESSIONALS ─────────

FOR PARENTS

The question facing the concerned, sometimes frantic, parents of an overweight teenager is what to do. I will identify three options.

Wait and See

The first strategy says take it easy. It maintains there is no danger, so why do anything. Your teenager likely will outgrow overweight, so leave him alone.

Yet for some parents, scientists, and practitioners (see later), wait and see is risky. For them, the fat child chances becoming the fat adult, and the fat teenager chances doing so even more. In his book, *The Pain of Obesity*, University of Pennsylvania psychiatrist Dr. Albert Stunkard writes:

> The odds against an obese child's being a normal-weight adult were more than four to one. And for those who did not reduce during adolescence, the odds may have been more than 28 to 1. (p. 182)[1]

Perhaps you reject the wait-and-see strategy because in your mind society makes overweight teenagers miserable.

To you, teenagers are put down for being heavy, see themselves as ugly, feel responsible for their plight, and derogate themselves cruelly.

Alternatively, you may find no evidence that your teenager is mean to himself. In fact, you are convinced that he feels little if any gloom, discomfort, or instability about who he is.

What do overweight teenagers think of themselves and other overweight teenagers? What do thin teenagers think of their overweight peers? To attempt to answer, we have interviewed hundreds of young persons in Canada, asking them in various ways what they like or dislike about fat people. We find that the hardest on the overweight are themselves overweight. Nonetheless, they feel okay about their own looks and personalities.

Yet, the heaviest teens we see in school halls and classrooms do not want to participate in our research. Why they do not, we do not know. We suspect it is because they believe we will label them and by so doing demean them, that as healthcare professionals we will fault them as perhaps their physicians already have done. If they did talk to us, maybe they would tell us that their peers brutalize them, their lives are unpleasant, and their looks and places in society are less than all right.

Promote Small Changes

Your teenager is overweight, but wants you to back off. She feels that her weight is her business and even if unhappy about it (and she may well be content) does not want you to dwell or focus on it. Tread gently. Talk to her about her feelings toward school and friends, and let her know you care. Talk to her about small gradual changes you would like to make to improve the family's nutrition, but unless medical reasons demand it, do not force on her sweeping dietary changes. Doing so will likely boomerang. Facing too many dietary prescriptions and proscriptions, she may rebel. She may more often snack and dine out of the home to dim the light on and prevent the inquiries about her foods. Try to interest her in family exercises: family walks, hikes, bike rides, swims.

Promote Large Changes

Your teenager is overweight and desires help. Table 4.3 names possible jobs for you:

- Help design or finance a program, or both.
- Help stock foods that make the program run smoother—foods low in fat and high in other nutrients for the calories they yield.
- Help create menus.
- Help arrange exercise opportunities.

Find out about his health, degree of overweight, and need for overweight control. Together, visit a physician to learn about calorie intake, immediate and future goals, and special needs for specific foods. Talk to your teenager about his commitment to, motivation for, and expectations of an overweight control program. Table 10.1 lists major concerns and questions to address.

Before beginning to help, you may wish to consult a professional specializing in overweight control, someone your physician recommends. I will outline what we at the Manitoba Obesity Center do.

TABLE 10.1. Questions and Concerns

- How healthy is my teen (including disease risks)?
- Percent overweight.
- Percent fat.
- Does my teen think he's too heavy and why?
- Does my teen say there's ridicule at school or at home, or both?
- Am I willing to commit myself to the extra work on my teen's behalf that an overweight control program needs?
- How committed is my teen to undergoing an overweight control program?
- Have I enlisted the support of my teen's relatives?
- What do I intend to do to support my teen's efforts to lessen overweight?
- What's unfair to my family about the program?
- If there's animosity in the home toward what my teen intends to do, what steps can I take to reduce this animosity?
- Have I consulted the family's physician?
- Have I consulted a weight control specialist, nutritionist, dietitian, physical educator?
- What are the body-change goals?
- What are the calorie intake goals at the start?
- What nutritional changes (e.g., fewer fatty foods) are needed?
- What are the activity goals?
- What behaviors need changing?

[a]Adapted from LeBow, M. D. (1991). *Overweight Children: Helping Your Child Achieve Lifetime Weight Control.* New York: Insight Books.

FOR PROFESSIONALS

We ask that the teenagers referred to us call before we schedule an appointment. Sometimes we get the call, sometimes not.

When we do, we explore motivation for change: what the teenager wants, whether she comes freely to us, whether she is willing to work at changing. If she wishes not to come in, we would support that decision—if there is no medical emergency, and usually there is not. As said, unless she wants it, therapy will likely fail, and when it does, she, her parents, and her physician may judge that she has failed again.

Because our first goal is helping teens feel better about themselves, we will counsel some to postpone or to avoid weight control therapy. Some teens, especially those with histories of yo-yo restrictive dieting, are unready for weight control treatment and will surely fail at it, denigrating themselves for having done so. Before we would ever target weight and fat, we would address body image and self-worth.

The Whole Person

Trained in clinical psychology that emphasizes behavior therapy, I used to welcome referrals from other clinical psychologists and psychiatrists who said something like this: "This patient has tics, fears, anxiety, panic, or obsessions and compulsions. I'm treating his depression; will you treat his (whatever) and leave the depression to me?"

Years ago, I naively bought that limit-care line. Now I reject it. I will treat particular problems, but I will not blind

myself to other dilemmas. Seldom does the young overweight man or woman need only what's initially re-
quested, overweight control. Other issues, some contribut-
ing to overweight, often need to be considered first. An
overweight, unhappy 17-year-old girl who binges when
she feels blue may profit from both of you uncovering her
cognitive distortions before targeting her overweight.

The Therapist

Therapists treating overweight teenagers should nurture,
magnify, and broaden small instances of progress. Therapists should be seen as genuine, warm, tuned-in, trustwor-
thy, and empathic. They should seize opportunities to
praise, rank highly the therapeutic relationship for promoting change, and inspire confidence. They should bring
to therapy knowledge of adolescent development and
thinking and knowledge of overweight control, including
nutrition, physiology, and behavior.

Framing the Issue

An overweight 16-year-old girl may tell us of turmoil in
her life:

> Everyone at school teases me about my body. Most of
> the time I avoid these people, but I wish I didn't have
> to. I never date. My parents aren't mean, but I know
> they hate my weight. Getting clothes is a problem.

She may tell us that her worth, chances of romance,
being liked, being loved, being happy are inversely related
to the number of extra pounds she carries. Typical dialogue:

THERAPIST: Do you think you're overweight?

TEENAGER: Yes, why would I come if I didn't?

THERAPIST: Do you think being overweight is why you're unhappy?

TEENAGER: You bet. Of course it is.

THERAPIST: And if you were thin, would you be content and have no more problems?

TEENAGER: Yes. I'm sure that I'd be much happier if only I were thin. If I fit in, better things would happen to me.

THERAPIST: It's true that most of us do get closer to the good things in life if we feel that we fit in.

TEENAGER: I just said that.

THERAPIST: Yes, but I want to clear up something. You seem to be implying that the good things in life happen only to those who are thin. It's unnecessary to be thin to feel that you've an important place in this world, one you're proud of and happy about. It's dangerous to think that only thin people are worthy.

TEENAGER: Why is it dangerous?

THERAPIST: Tying worthiness to thinness may lead you to starve or to binge and then to vomit just to get thin, and those practices are more likely to get you sick than they are anything else. You may come to think that a thin body is what's right—the thinner the better. And that idea is wrong. Many anorexics, those who try to emaciate themselves, learn the hard way it's wrong. How you feel and think about yourself is what counts, not thinness.

TEENAGER: A thin body is the best body. Are you saying that losing weight is wrong?

THERAPIST: Not really. But losing weight isn't always the same thing as losing overweight. You can get less overweight and not lose any weight, if you get taller. And you can get less overweight and not lose any weight simply by getting older. All this will become clear later. Right now, however, I just want you to hear that being thinner won't automatically make you happier. Thinness doesn't equal happiness. Control overweight, if that's what you want. But thinness isn't the Royal Road to never-ending bliss.

In brief, framing the issue often involves injecting the teenager with a dose of reality.

Jobs, Goals, Quitting

After hearing that losing weight isn't the magic for joy, the teenager may want out. Some leave when they learn we need them to keep records. "Too much like school. Don't you have diet pills?" Even though we supply bound printed forms to make recording easier, more than just a few teens, hating the active role we request, say goodbye. A few quit because of goals, wanting fast loss, not slow or no loss.

Some others quit later, losing interest along the way. As Chapter 9 describes, they may leave for one of several reasons: treatment causes friction in the family, treatment is viewed as worthless and silly, efforts go unsupported at home. Moreover, they may quit because the therapist fails to praise their efforts or because they feel that they are mismatched in the therapy group. (A girl 80 pounds overweight in a treatment group of girls 22–33 pounds overweight may quit, feeling apart in weight, attractiveness, and opportunities. Large disparities in age likewise may cause the older or younger teenager to feel out of place.)

Success

Most important to teenagers is success. Unfortunately, we cannot guarantee it. All we have is a rational approach, helpful to some, unhelpful to some. No one, we tell our patients, has the healthful, universal cure. We promise to collaborate with them to search for workable, sensible, and efficient answers.

Failure

Teenagers equate failure with weakness, casting stones at themselves when overweight leaves too slowly or stays. They cement self-worth to society's dictum to be thin, at all costs be thin. Believing looks and worth are one and the same, they put shape in charge of self-esteem. And when the body will not cooperate with the belief in what is good, proper, and attractive, self-esteem suffers. Therefore, we make certain they understand the following:

> Controlling overweight, eating, and exercising isn't something you can just make up your mind to do, *will* to happen. Don't damn yourself and say you lack willpower when plans go awry. Doing so not only hurts pride but also derails searches for situations, actions, and thoughts that need attention. Willpower answers, pseudoanswers, say that internal weakness explains failure. Willpower analyses explain passively, blame incorrectly, accuse unfairly.

> In contrast, responsibility analyses explain actively. They seek observable changes: Buy fewer rich foods; visit the bakery less often; play basketball, football, volleyball more often; watch less TV; avoid rigid

diets to avoid self-defeating hunger. Search not for flaws of character, but for changes of behavior.

We want our patients to know that program failure reveals therapist ignorance more than patient weakness and to realize that willpower interpretations of failure are fruitless, demeaning, and distracting.

Backup

Dietitians improve overweight therapy for teens needing to avoid or to eat particular foods. Physical education specialists improve it for teens needing particular exercises and tests of conditioning. There are other health professionals who can assist the overweight teenager.

Physicians, mentioned throughout this book, must from the start of the teen's treatment be involved. We trust our patients to tell us of the effects on them (good and bad) of what they do, and they trust us to give correct, competent advice. But, especially before treatment, there is much they cannot tell us, nor we them. That's why, prior to it, we ask each teenager to have a physician complete Table 10.2. It alerts us to dietary and exercise proscriptions, chronic ailments, and other medical conditions. It alerts the physician to the program, including initial calorie intake. To set it, we rely on the RDA energy levels (Table 2.1) and a seven-day or more baseline of eating (Figure 5.1).

Interview

We also rely on the teenager's estimate, obtained from an interview, of which level is comfortable. What's more, as shown in Table 10.3, we ask about health, demography,

TABLE 10.2. Physician Input Form

Teenager's name _____ **Date**_____

The above wishes to become less overweight. The program to be applied includes eating better, exercising, and life-style change. Please inform us if there is any medical reason that the above named person should not undergo this program or if there are any medical concerns you have about what we intend to do. Calorie intake will be set at _____ initially.

According to my knowledge, there is no medical reason or reasons that would prevent the person named from participating.

Physician's signature _____

Date _____

For information about the program please call:

Therapist's name_____

Phone_____

TABLE 10.3. Overweight Teenager Interview[a]

Teen's name _____Date _____

Address & phone _____

Date of birth _____

Height _____in.

Weight _____lb.

BMI _____

Right arm skinfold _____

Waist size _____

Hips size _____

Ratio of waist to hips [W/H] _____

Other Circumferences _____

_____

_____

_____

Information on parents (obtained from parents)

    Relationship to teen: Biological or adoptive

    Mother's occupation _____

    Father's occupation _____

    Years of schooling: Mother _____Father _____

    Approximate annual family income _____

Questions about the teen's history (obtained from teen)

  1. When were you first overweight?

  2. Who else in your family is overweight?

  3. Have you tried to reduce before?

  —How many times?

  —About how long does one of your tries last?

  —Why did you stop the last time you tried?

  4. Have you gained weight in the last month?

  5. Have you ever been in a hospital?

  —If yes, why?

Questions about eating

6. Do you like to eat?
7. Name up to five foods you like the most.
8. Name up to five foods you dislike the most.
9. Do you ever have a snack? (If yes, go on)
   —How often a day do you snack?
   —What do you have for snacks?
   —When (time) during a day do you snack?
   —What snack foods are there at home?
   —When you snack, what are you doing other than eating?
10. What's in a good dinner?
11. How many meals do you have a day other than snacks?
12. Do you buy or bring your lunch to school or go home for lunch?
13. Do you ever buy desserts at school or near the school?
14. Do you buy food or bring it when you go to the movies?
    —If yes, what?
15. When you're shopping, do you stop for something to eat?
16. When you watch television, do you eat?
17. When you study, do you eat?
18. Do you ever eat without thinking about it?

Questions about activity

19. Do you play sports? (If yes, go on)
    —How often?
    —What usually?
    —Who usually plays with you?
20. How long each day on the average do you watch television?

TABLE 10.3. *Continued*

21. Do you have a bike to use? (If yes, go on)
    —How many times a week do you ride and for how long each time?
22. Do you go swimming once or more per week?
23. Do you roller-skate or ice-skate once or more per week?
24. Do you play tennis once or more per week?
25. What other activities (recreations and exercises) do you do once or more per week?
26. How do you generally get to school? (mode of transportation)

Questions about peers, society, and shape
27. Do others tease you about your weight? (If yes, go on)
    —In what ways?
    —How often?
    —What sorts of things do they say?
28. Are you included in social plans?
29. Does your teacher ever say nasty things to you or about overweight people in general?
30. What sorts of things do your parent(s) say about your being overweight?
31. What do your brothers and/or sisters say about it?
32. What does the doctor say about it?
33. Is it healthier to be overweight or underweight?
34. Can you ever be too thin?
35. Are people nasty to overweight people?

How I feel about me
36. Are you . . . ? (Circle each the teen answers "yes" to.)
    clean, kind, mean, smart, weak, honest, fat, lonely, lazy, strong, sad, sloppy, a fast runner, heavy, happy, a slow runner, not smart, brave, ugly, thin, healthy, afraid, good-looking, muscular, curvy

TABLE 10.3. *Continued*

37. Do you think you are a leader?
38. Do you feel as if your clothes are tight on you?
39. Do you have one or more good friends?

Questions about double messages

Message: Food splendor, fat ugly

40. How often in a week's time are you told by mother and/or father that it's bad to be overweight?
41. How often in a week's time do brothers and/or sisters tell you it's bad to be overweight?
42. At your house, what does a typical dinner consist of?
43. At your house, what does a fancy dinner consist of?
   —How often do you think in the last month you had fancy dinners?

Message: Clean plate if want dessert, fat is due to sweets

44. How often in a week's time are you told that food is precious, so you shouldn't waste it?
45. How often in a week's time are you told to think of those who are starving—those not as lucky as you?
46. How often in a week's time are you told that eating candy, pie, ice cream, cookies, or cake makes you heavy?
47. Are you told by your parents that you overeat?
48. To get dessert, do you have to finish your lunch or dinner? (If yes, go on)
   —How often does this happen in a week, typically?

Message: Play with us, we don't like fatsos

49. Are you ever chosen to play team sports?
50. Do teachers encourage you to play team sports?
51. How likely is it that you will be last choice on a team?
52. Are you good at team sports?
53. Do you play team sports during or after the school day?

TABLE 10.3. *Continued*

Message: Eat to be friendly, friends aren't fat
54. Do you join friends at restaurants or coffeeshops?
55. When with friends, do you ever eat to be sociable?
56. When with friends, is it difficult to eat better?
57. When with friends, are you concerned they'll know you're trying to eat more sensibly?
58. Do your friends make jokes about overweight people?
59. When with friends, do you usually eat just because they do?

*a*Some questions in the double message section are adapted from Rallo (1982). Others from LeBow (1981, 1991).

TABLE 10.3. *Continued*

overweight history, eating, activity, perceptions of self, and double messages. Multisectioned and primarily open-ended, the interview takes several hours to complete; we space it over several sessions.

Throughout treatment, we usually have parents help in therapy—sometimes, as Yale psychologist Dr. Kelly Brownell and colleagues do,[2] seeing parents separately from their teens and sometimes, as University of Pennsylvania psychologist Dr. Thomas Wadden and colleagues do,[3] with their teens. However we include parents and whatever roles we teach, we try to stop them from forcing compliance and unfairly derogating lapses in compliance. Our aim is having parents encourage change. Also throughout treatment, we explain terms such as calories, weight, fat, and so forth, as we draw procedures from several available programs.

Programs

No one treatment package addresses all problems for all teens. We borrow to tailor from these regimens:

Learn

Developed for adults as well as for youths, the Learn program of Dr. Brownell includes 86 tactics. "Learn" means "L" for life-style—31 techniques, including monitoring and stimulus control. It also means "E" for exercise—14 techniques, "A" for attitude—19 techniques, "R" for relationship—10 techniques, and "N" for nutrition—12 techniques.[4]

Action

Frances Berg, a North Dakota social scientist and home economist, directs this program to youths in school and to those working. She addresses how they diet, exercise, and live. Her focus on life-style change, good nutrition, and exercise downplays both dieting and losing weight. She encourages aerobics, record-keeping, avoiding snacks for awhile, and enlisting help from others. Methods include contracting, better attitudes toward oneself, fighting binge-ing, and improving eating. Wealthy in ideas, "Action" stands for activity, creativity, touching others, identity, omitting no meals, and no snacking (control snacking).[5]

Treating Childhood and Adolescent Obesity

Like the two programs just named, this one employs multipart lessons on self-monitoring, stimulus control, and thinking better. Besides these, the lessons talk of setting goals, contracting, reinforcement, learning to say no to food friends and to waiters. Its authors, Drs. Daniel Kirschenbaum, William Johnson, and Peter Stalonas, write to help therapists plan and enact therapy. Targeting exercise, they separate activities into light, moderate, and heavy; youths track the calories expended. As well, the authors target eating via exchange dieting.[6]

Habits and Shape

This is University of California nutrition educator Joanne Ikeda's older program for teenagers. In it, she emphasizes commitment, helpers, and life-style. Also, she illustrates calisthenics youths may do.[7]

Shapedown

"Shapedown," about 15 years old, comprehensively treats overweight teens. Targeting weight, eating, activity, feelings, communication, and social interactions, it seeks small, gradual, and livable changes. Often, parents play helper roles. Developed by Laurel Mellin, a registered dietitian at the School of Medicine, University of California, San Francisco, "Shapedown" is offered across the nation. There are workbooks for practitioners and training materials for teens and parents. "Shapedown" seems effective.[8]

FOR PARENTS AND PROFESSIONALS: HEALTH CONCERNS

Because questions of whether overweight teenagers are unhealthy concern parents, health professionals, and politicians, attempts to answer abound. But answers remain elusive, and investigators disagree.

Some scientists claim that one day soon the over-weight teen will be large enough to wear the clothes of the seriously overweight adult. Indeed, Dr. Steven Gortmaker of Harvard and colleagues note that the fattest adults once were fat teenagers. Say these researchers:

> Because adults obese in adolescence are overrepre-sented among the severely obese, we predict that the severity of adult obesity will also increase substan-tially. (p. 539)[9]

To assert who's too heavy, scientists use tables of average and desirable weights. They also use the body mass index (BMI).

$$\text{Body mass index} = \text{weight in kilograms}/\text{height in meters}^2$$

It correlates well with body fat. Teens with a BMI greater than 30 are thought to be overweight.[10] Adults with a BMI of 25–30 are considered overweight and those with a BMI greater than 30, obese; categorizations differ among re-searchers. In the book *Promoting Healthy Weights,* Canadian health officials translate healthy and unhealthy weights into BMI ranges.[11] Each range or zone indicates risks of falling into that BMI range: Reaching zone A, BMI less than 20, is risky; falling into zone D, BMI more than 27, also is risky. Low and high BMIs, underweight and overweight, are undesirable. Between 20 and 25 is thought to be good.

Those who attempt to alarm with their argument that the overweight teenager is soon to be the overweight adult presume that there is something wrong with being an overweight adult. What is wrong, they claim, is that the overweight adult is unhealthy.

The Health of the Overweight Adult

There is evidence that being overweight when over age 21 connects with a devastating array of ills. Excess pounds correlate with arteriosclerosis, hypertension, maturity-onset diabetes, toxemias of pregnancy, gallbladder disease, low back pain, osteoarthritis of the hips and knees, dermatological problems, surgical problems, and more. Scrutinizing data from large-scale surveys of the health of Americans, Dr. Theodore Van Itallie of Columbia University Department of Medicine finds that the risk of hypertension is three times greater if the adult is overweight than if not.[12] Losing weight helps the hypertensive person because losing mitigates what Dr. Franz Messerli of the Ochsner Clinic in New Orleans calls the double burden of obesity and high blood pressure on the heart. He says:

> However since both obesity and hypertension increase cardiac workload, although by different mechanisms, their presence in the same patient results in a double burden to the left ventricle. (p. 1077)[13]

Hypercholesterolemia (high cholesterol) risk also is pronounced for the overweight adult. Dr. Van Itallie explains:

> The relative risk of hypercholesterolemia for overweight Americans aged 20 to 75 years is 1.5 times that of those who are not overweight. (p. 986)[14]

The difference between the heavy and not-so-heavy regarding this danger is even greater at younger ages—20 to

45 years. He also reveals that the overweight compared with the nonoverweight are more likely to contract non-insulin-dependent diabetes mellitus.

As well, heaviness heightens the likelihood of the perils of coronary heart disease and cancer. Francis Berg in *Health Risks of Obesity* notes that coronary heart disease is the number one killer of Americans and that stroke ranks as killer number three.[15]

About cancer, indicates Dr. Artemis Simopoulos of the Center on Genetics, Nutrition, and Health, obese males run a greater risk (compared with thinner peers) of perishing from cancer of the prostate, colon, and rectum.[16] Overweight females, according to the National Institutes of Health Consensus Development Panel, run a greater risk (compared with thinner peers) of dying from cancer of the breast, gallbladder, uterus, biliary passages, and ovaries.[17]

Such data lead experts, fewer today than years ago, to advise overweight adults to reduce. The National Institutes of Health says that even 20% overweight requires treatment. The more overweight, the more urgency; losing when extremely overweight, defined by that group as being 100 or more pounds overweight, may be "lifesaving."[18] Being overweight lowers life expectancy, risks disease, and exacerbates health problems; if overweight is removed, risk factor profiles improve.

But today, believing that extra pounds in adulthood impacts disastrously on morbidity (illness) and on mortality (death) and that losing weight saves lives and improves health are challenged. Declare researchers Drs. David Garner of Michigan State and Susan Wooley of the University of Cincinnati in their review paper:

It is difficult to find any scientific justification for the continued use of dietary treatments of obesity. (p. 767)[19]

About taking off the weight, Frances Berg in *The Health Risks of Weight Loss* says:

Some interventions appear benign; others entail risks much greater than the risks of overweight. (Introduction)[20]

The Health of the Overweight Adolescent

What role does body weight play in the physical well-being of teenagers? Is losing weight what these youths need to do? Dr. Patricia Castiglia of the State University of New York at Buffalo School of Nursing comments:

Although there is a low mortality incidence associated with obesity in childhood and adolescence, the morbidity rates are high (p. 221)[21]

Dr. Wadden and colleagues echo this, concluding that overweight teenagers are more likely than nonoverweight ones to be hypertensive and hypercholesteremic.[22] Dr. Albert Rocchini of the University of Minnesota Medical Center indicates that over 95% of the obese teenagers in one study showed such risks for cardiovascular disease as lowered high density lipoprotein cholesterol (often called the good cholesterol), raised blood pressure, heightened triglycerides in the blood, and high total cholesterol.[23] Teenage obesity figures into this risk, says Dr. Rocchini, by affecting hyperlipidemia, hypertension, and glucose intolerance.

Will weight loss help? Dr. Martin Wabitsch of the University of Ulm and colleagues in Germany suggest that it might, particularly among teenage girls with an abdominal (apple shape) type of obesity, the type associated with cardiovascular problems in adults. They write:

> ... our finding of a preferential diminution of the abdominal fat depots during weight reduction is promising ... (p. 910)[24]

A number of other scientists and practitioners, such as Dr. Rocchini and Dr. Wadden, also would argue that treatment benefits. High blood pressures and lipid abnormalities respond well to weight reductions; notes Dr. Rocchini, exercise, especially, improves health.

> ... when weight loss was incorporated with physical conditioning, the greatest decrease in resting systolic blood pressure and heart rate was observed. (p. 236)[25]

What's the future for the overweight teenager? As said, some untreated overweight teens may become severely overweight adults. But even if they do not, and there is no guarantee they will, there may be later health problems, as a result of earlier heaviness.

Dr. Aviva Must of the U.S. Department of Agriculture Human Nutrition Research Center on Aging at Tufts University and colleagues describe how earlier weight affects later health.[26] Evaluating 55-year follow-up data gathered on hundreds of participants of the *Third Harvard Growth*

Study conducted from 1922 to 1935, she and her group document that teenage overweight correlates with adult disease and death.

To do so, she looked at the records of 508 men and women who had either died, become ill, or remained well since being included in the study decades earlier. She made greater than the 75th percentile body mass index her cutoff for overweight. Men and women who had had a body mass index greater than the 75th percentile for two year-long periods sometime between their 13th and 18th years (adolescence) were called overweight. Those who had had a body mass index falling between the 25th and 50th percentiles during these teen years were called lean.

Dr. Must then correlated these past overweight and lean groups with later mortality and morbidity data available at the 1988 follow-up. Over 30% of the original participants had died. Survivors had reached, on average, 73 years of age.

Many more men overweight as teenagers than not overweight then had died from combined illnesses and from coronary heart disease. Colorectal cancer and stroke also had claimeᴗ the lives of such men. Morbidity data (e.g., heart disease and atherosclerosis) for both sexes also reflected this adolescent-overweight-adult-disaster finding.

The mortality results for the women were unlike those for the men. Perhaps as Dr. George Bray of the Pennington Biomedical Research Center in Louisiana suggests, had Dr. Must set the criterion of overweight (the cutoff) higher, she might have found many of the same startling results for the women that she did for the men.[27] Dr. Must did show that those adult females overweight as adolescents compared with those not overweight at that time were more likely to suffer arthritis and difficulties climbing stairs, lifting, and walking a quarter mile—daily routines.

What's more, she found that although over half of the overweight teens were currently overweight adults, only for those with diabetes did overweight in adulthood impact negatively. So, except for diabetes, the adult body mass index did not contribute much to her findings on death and disease. It was the earlier body mass index, the one during the long since past teenage years, that had the sweeping catastrophic effect.

She calls for increased attention to preventing overweight during the teen years.

> ... the prevention of overweight in childhood and adolescence may be the most effective means of decreasing the associated mortality and morbidity in adults. (p. 1354)[28]

In an interview with writer Jane Brody of *The New York Times,* she warns against weight cycling. Also, she advocates lessening fat in the teenage diet, diminishing sit-down activities, and increasing chances for exercise.[29] More than weight losses, these life-style changes are often the best treatment targets.

Promote reductions in pounds delicately and do not, as so many adolescents would have you do, rush into making them happen. Do not accept weight loss as the undeniably best solution to the physical woes of the overweight teen. Frequently, as explained, reducing is not right for a growing teenager. Also, lost pounds are not the direct measures of a change in health; better are improvements in blood pressure, in lipid abnormalities, in metabolic derangements, and in fat patterning (e.g., lessening upper body fat).

A philosophy of losing at all costs feeds society's demeaning edict—be thin or else—a decree that helps spawn anorexia and bulimia. A philosophy of losing at all costs encourages unwholesome, ineffective, silly, and dangerous weight control stratagems: fasting, restrictive dieting, weight cycling, taking diet pills, denying oneself basic nutrition (see Chapter 3). A philosophy of losing at all costs can ultimately lower the teenager's self-esteem.

Promote sensible eating and exercising. Cultivate these ends by helping teenagers modify their environments in the ways this book puts forth. And stop them from frenzy dieting where, as partner in a shape-condemning society, you portray their extra calories as nails that will some day seal their psychological and physical coffins.

AFTERWORD ────────────────

You've been on a journey to learn about the mysterious and intractable condition of overweight. Your travels have led to concepts like energy and fat, practices like stimulus control and thinking better, and obstacles like "never again" commandments and inactivity beliefs. Also, your travels have led to warnings:

- Don't begin overweight control without first thinking hard about whether and why it is something you want now.
- Don't attempt overweight control before consulting a physician. Find out if you need it. Find out what to target.
- Don't start overweight control believing that to fail now is to fail forever.
- Don't misconstrue program failure as personal failure. Ask what parts did not work and why they did not. Look for answers in strategies and situations. Attack programs, not teenage programmers.
- Don't alone try overweight control. Collaborate with parents and friends.
- Don't weight-cycle.

- Don't flirt with the bizarre: fasting, fad dieting, starving–stuffing, denying excessively, yo-yo dieting, diet pill popping, bingeing–purging.
- Don't forget exercise.

Practice self-control. When buying carrots, apples, and oranges so snacks contain fewer cookies, candies, and waffles, when taping notes inside your school locker to remember it's volleyball after school, when taking the tailored steps to well-being, you are doing self-control. Methods espoused in this book, such as contracting, using positives, and the rest, will help you self-control.

Regulate overweight if you wish to, but do so not by throwing out good sense—not by eating poorly, not by exercising exhaustingly. Be rational. Be fair. Be kind.

Control eating and activity to take charge of yourself, not to worship some fickle image of good looks, for after bowing to that graven image you may stand up starved and sick. Feel good about who you are. Worth cannot be weighed on a weight scale.

NUTRIENTS FOR ALL ────────

The table on the following pages is taken from *Recommended Dietary Allowances*, © 1989, by the National Academy of Sciences, National Academy Press, Washington, D.C.

Food and Nutrition Board, National Academy of Sciences–National Research Council Recommended Dietary Allowances, Revised 1989 (designed for the Maintenance of Good Nutrition of Practically All Healthy People in the United States)[a]

Category	Age (years) or condition	Weight[b] (kg)	(lb)	Height[b] (cm)	(in)	Protein (g)
Infants	0.0–0.5	6	13	60	24	13
	0.5–1.0	9	20	71	28	14
Children	1–3	13	29	90	35	16
	4–6	20	44	112	44	24
	7–10	28	62	132	52	28
Males	11–14	45	99	157	62	45
	15–18	66	145	176	69	59
	19–24	72	160	177	70	58
	25–50	79	174	176	70	63
	51+	77	170	173	68	63
Females	11–14	46	101	157	62	46
	15–18	55	120	163	64	44
	19–24	58	128	164	65	46
	25–50	63	138	163	64	50
	51+	65	143	160	63	50
Pregnant						60
Lactating	1st 6 months					65
	2nd 6 months					62

[a]The allowances, expressed as average daily intakes over time, are intended to provide for individual variations among most normal persons as they live in the United States under usual environmental stresses. Diets should be based on a variety of common foods in order to provide other nutrients for which human requirements have been less well defined.

Category	Vitamin A (µg RE)[c]	Vitamin D (µg)[d]	Vitamin E (mg α-TE)[e]	Vitamin K (µg)
Infants	375	7.5	3	5
	375	10	4	10
Children	400	10	6	15
	500	10	7	20
	700	10	7	30
Males	1,000	10	10	45
	1,000	10	10	65
	1,000	10	10	70
	1,000	5	10	80
	1,000	5	10	80
Females	800	10	8	45
	800	10	8	55
	800	10	8	60
	800	5	8	65
	800	5	8	65
Pregant	800	10	10	65
Lactating	1,300	10	12	65
	1,200	10	11	65

[b]Weights and heights of Reference Adults are actual medians for the U.S. population of the designated age, as reported by NHANES II. The median weights and heights of those under 19 years of age were taken from Hamill et al. (1979). The use of these figures does not imply that the height-to-weight ratios are ideal.

[c]Retinol equivalents. 1 retinol equivalent = 1 µg retinol or 6 µg β-carotene.

[d]As cholecalciferol. 10µg cholecalciferol = 400 IU of vitamin D.

[e]α-Tocopherol equivalents. 1 mg d-α tocopherol = 1 α-TE.

Category	Vitamin C (mg)	Thiamin (mg)	Riboflavin (mg)	Niacin (mg NE)[f]
Infants	30	0.3	0.4	5
	35	0.4	0.5	6
Children	40	0.7	0.8	9
	45	0.9	1.1	12
	45	1.0	1.2	13
Males	50	1.3	1.5	17
	60	1.5	1.8	20
	60	1.5	1.7	19
	60	1.5	1.7	19
	60	1.2	1.4	15
Females	50	1.1	1.3	15
	60	1.1	1.3	15
	60	1.1	1.3	15
	60	1.1	1.3	15
	60	1.0	1.2	13
Pregnant	70	1.5	1.6	17
Lactating	95	1.6	1.8	20
	90	1.6	1.7	20

[f] 1 NE (niacin equivalent) is equal to 1 mg of niacin or 60 mg of dietary tryptophan.

Category	Vita-min B$_6$ (mg)	Folate (µg)	Vita-min B$_{12}$ (µg)	Calcium (mg)	Phos-phorus (mg)
Infants	0.3	25	0.3	400	300
	0.6	35	0.5	600	500
Children	1.0	50	0.7	800	800
	1.1	75	1.0	800	800
	1.4	100	1.4	800	800
Males	1.7	150	2.0	1,200	1,200
	2.0	200	2.0	1,200	1,200
	2.0	200	2.0	1,200	1,200
	2.0	200	2.0	800	800
	2.0	200	2.0	800	800
Females	1.4	150	2.0	1,200	1,200
	1.5	180	2.0	1,200	1,200
	1.6	180	2.0	1,200	1,200
	1.6	180	2.0	800	800
	1.6	180	2.0	800	800
Pregnant	2.2	400	2.2	1,200	1,200
Lactating	2.1	280	2.6	1,200	1,200
	2.1	260	2.6	1,200	1,200

Category	Magne- sium (mg)	Iron (mg)	Zinc (mg)	Iodine (µg)	Selenium (µg)
Infants	40	6	5	40	10
	60	10	5	50	15
Children	80	10	10	70	20
	120	10	10	90	20
	170	10	10	120	30
Males	270	12	15	150	40
	400	12	15	150	50
	350	10	15	150	70
	350	10	15	150	70
	350	10	15	150	70
Females	280	15	12	150	45
	300	15	12	150	50
	280	15	12	150	55
	280	15	12	150	55
	280	10	12	150	55
Pregnant	320	30	15	175	65
Lactating	355	15	19	200	75
	340	15	16	200	75

TYPICAL FOODS ━━━━━

APPROXIMATE CALORIES AND FAT[a]

Food	Calories (for 3½ oz. or other indicated portion size)	Grams of fat
Apple (small)	56	0.6
Artichoke (hearts)	26	0.4
Asparagus (whole spears, cooked)	23	0.2
Bacon (fried, drained)		
Canadian	278	17.5
Strips	595	51
Banana (raw)	80	0.2
Beans		
Green (boiled)	25	0.2
Kidney (cooked)	117	0.5
Lima (cooked)	137	0.6
Bologna	298	27
Bread		
White (slice)	65	0.7
Wheat (slice)	57	0.7
Broccoli (boiled, drained)	28	0.3
Butter (tsp)	35	4

Food	Calories (for 3½ oz. or other indicated portion size)	Grams of fat
Cake		
Angel food	278	0.2
Chocolate layer	328	17.7
Gingerbread	300	10
Pound cake	410	19
Candy		
Caramel (plain)	396	10+
Chocolate peanuts	557	41
Granola bar (1 bar)	120	5
Milk chocolate	530	35+
Cantaloupe	28	0.1
Carrots (raw)	42	0.2
Cashews (shelled, roasted)	567	46
Catsup	109	3+
Cauliflower (fresh)	27	0.2
Celery	15	0.1
Cereals (ready-to-eat)		
Oat Squares (30 g)	118	1.3
Life (30 g)	118	1.8
Rice Krispies (30 g)	110	0.1
Granola (30 g)	120	6+
Cheese		
American (processed)	370	30
Cheddar	397	32.2
Cottage (creamed)	105	4.2
Cottage (uncreamed)	85	0.3
Swiss (processed)	357	27
Cheese spread (processed)	278	20.7
Cherries	70	0.3
Chewing gum (reg. 1 stick)	9	0

Food	Calories (for 3½ oz. or other indicated portion size)	Grams of fat
Chicken		
Broiled meat	137	3.8
Potpie	231	13.5
Cookies (plain)	494	20.8
Corn	82	1.0
Corned beef (cooked)	375	30.4
Crab (steamed without shell)	89	1.9
Cucumber (raw, without skin)	15	0.1
Cupcakes (plain, one 30 g)	106	3.6
Doughnuts		
Cake (plain, one 30 g)	117	5.6
Powdered (one 30 g)	155	9
Eggs		
Fried	217	17.2
Scrambled (milk added)	175	13
Fish		
Flounder	202	8.2
Halibut	170	7
Lobster (cooked meat)	95	1.5
Salmon (canned, red sockeye)	170	9.3
Salmon (broiled)	180	7.4
Scallops	109	1.4
Shrimp (fried with bread crumbs, batter)	228	10.9
Tuna (canned, packed in oil & drained)	195	8.1
Tuna (canned, packed in water)	125	0.8
Grapefruit (raw, pulp)	40	0.1
Grapes (raw with seeds and stems)	65	0.9
Gum (see Chewing gum)		

Food	Calories	Grams of fat
	(for 3½ oz. or other indi-cated portion size)	
Gumdrops (2 oz)	194	0.4
Ham (roasted)		
Lean and fat	385	32
Lean only	250	14
Hamburger		
Ground beef (lean, cooked)	218	11.2
Ground round (lean, cooked)	187	6
Honey	298	0
Ice cream		
12% fat	205	12.4
16% fat	220	16
Ice milk	149	5
Jelly beans	360	0.5
Kale (cooked)	40	0.7
Lamb		
Chops (loin, lean, cooked)	189	7.5
Shoulder (roasted, lean, no bone)	203	9.9
Lettuce (raw)	10	0.1
Liver (beef, fried)	228	10.6
Luncheon meat		
Boiled ham	228	16.6
Salami (beef)	180	13.5
Macaroni (cooked 10 min.)	149	0.5
Margarine (reg. 1 tsp)	30	3.3
Meat loaf	198	13.1
Milk		
whole (3.5%) (cup)	160	8.6
2% (cup)	135	4.8
1% (cup)	105	2.8
Skim (cup)	90	0.4
Mushrooms (raw, whole, untrimmed)	27	0.3

Food	Calories	Grams of fat
	(for 3½ oz. or other indi-	
	cated portion size)	
Mustard (tsp)	4	0.2
Noodles (egg, cooked)	119	1.4
Oranges (raw, peeled)	49	0.2
Peach (raw)	39	0.1
Peanut butter	595	50.6
Peanuts (roasted)	580	48.5
Pears (raw)	60	0.4
Pizza (cheese)	236	8.3
Plums (damson)	63	Trace
Pop (see Soft drinks)		
Popcorn (popped plain)	385	5
Potatoes (cooked)		
Baked in skin	89	0.1
Boiled in skin	79	0.1
French fried	268	12.9
Raisins	288	0.2
Rice (cooked, long grain)	103	0.1
Sausage (pork, cooked)	476	44.2
Soft drinks		
Colas (12 oz)	130	0
Ginger ale (12 oz)	135	0
Root beer (12 oz)	145	0
Seven-Up (12 oz)	145	0
Soup		
Chicken consomme (cup)	45	0.2
Cream of chicken (cup)	115	9.2
Sour cream (tsp)	9	0.8
Spaghetti (cooked 15 min)	109	0.4
Spareribs (pork, cooked)		
Fatty	466	42.5
Lean	407	35

Food	Calories Grams of fat (for 3½ oz. or other indicated portion size)	
Spinach (raw, untrimmed)	26	0.3
Steak (beef, broiled, lean)		
Club	450	40.2
Porterhouse	446	39.7
T-bone	440	39
Sirloin	350	27.2
Strawberries (raw, trimmed)	37	0.5
Tomato (raw, unpeeled)	22	0.2
Turkey (roasted)		
Meat and skin	220	9.5
Light meat only	179	3.9
Dark meat only	200	8.2
Veal loin (cooked, medium fat)	238	13.6
Watermelon	26	0.2
Yogurt (plain partially skimmed)	50–60	1.7–2

[a]Sources: B. Kraus (1979). *Calories and Carbohydrates.* New York: Grosset & Dunlap; E. Chabeck (1979). *The Complete Calorie Counter.* New York: Dell; C. Netzer and E. Chaback (1979). *Brand-Name Calorie Counter* (Abridged). New York: Dell; R. M. Deutsch (1978). *The Fat Counter Guide.* Palo Alto, CA: Bull Publishing; J. A. T. Pennington and H. Nichols Church (1980). *Food Values of Portions Commonly Used* (13th ed.) New York: Harper & Row; B. K. Watt and A. L. Merrill (1975). *Composition of Foods* (Agriculture Handbook No. 8, U.S. Department of Agriculture). Washington, DC: U.S. Government Printing Office.

GROWTH PERCENTILES ———

The graphs on the following pages were adapted from Hamill, P. V. V., Drizd, T. A., Johnson, C. L., Reed, R. B., Roche, A. F., and Moore, W. M. (1979). Physical growth: National Center for Health Statistics Percentiles. *Am. J. Clin. Nutr. 32*, 607–629. Data from the National Center for Health Statistics (NCHS), Hyattsville, Maryland. © 1980 Ross Laboratories. Used with permission of Ross Laboratories.

BOYS: 2 TO 18 YEARS   NAME_____   RECORD #_____

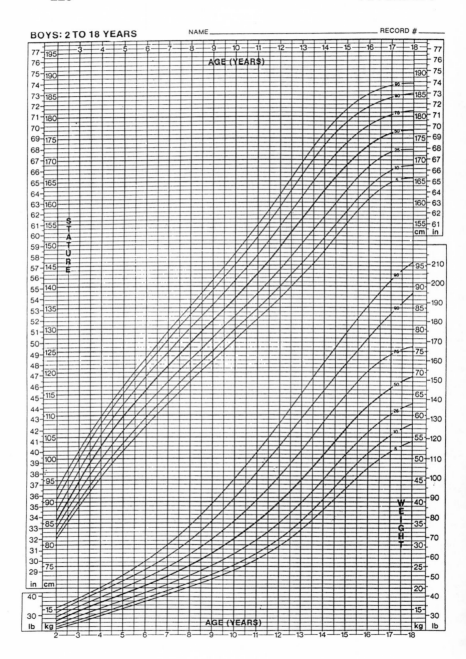

GIRLS: 2 TO 18 YEARS

NAME_____ RECORD #_____

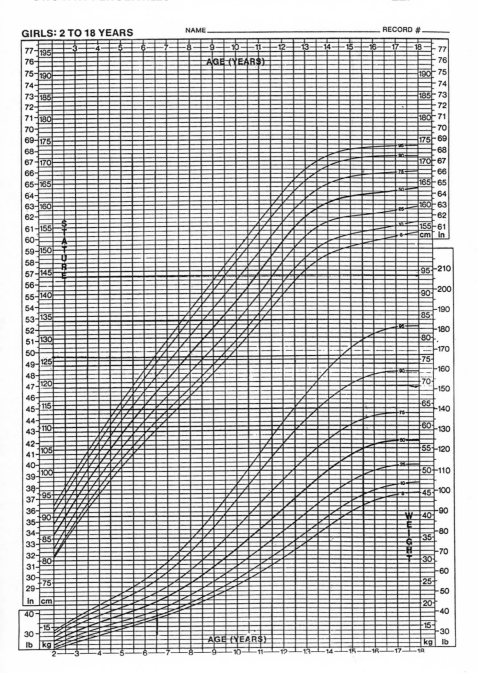

METRIC CONVERTER ⎯⎯⎯⎯

GRAMS TO OUNCES

Multiply number of grams in question by 0.035 to get ounces. For example, 200 grams is 7 ounces—200 grams × 0.035 equals 7 ounces.

$$\text{grams} \times 0.035 \text{ ounces}$$

OUNCES TO GRAMS

Multiply number of ounces in question by 28.35 to get grams. For example, 3 ounces is 85 grams—3 ounces × 28.35 equals 85 grams.

$$\text{ounces} \times 28.35 \text{ grams}$$

KILOGRAMS TO POUNDS

Multiply number of kilograms in question by 2.2 to get pounds. For example, 50 kilograms is 110 pounds—50 kilograms × 2.2 equals 110 pounds.

$$\text{kilograms} \times 2.2 \text{ pounds}$$

POUNDS TO KILOGRAMS

Multiply number of pounds in question by 0.454 to get kilograms. For example, 110 pounds is about 50 kilograms—110 pounds × 0.454 equals about 50 kilograms.

pounds × 0.454 kilogram

CENTIMETERS TO INCHES

Multiply number of centimeters in question by 0.394 to get inches. For example, 50 centimeters is 19.7 inches—50 centimeters × 0.394 equals 19.7 inches.

centimeters × 0.394 inch

INCHES TO CENTIMETERS

Multiply number of inches in question by 2.54 to get centimeters. For example, 20 inches is 50.8 centimeters—20 inches × 2.54 equals 50.8 centimeters.

inches × 2.54 centimeters

READINGS RECOMMENDED —

GENERAL INFORMATION ABOUT THE TEEN YEARS

Berger, K. S. (1991). *The Developing Person Through Childhood and Adolescence.* New York: Worth Publishers.

Santrock, J. W. (1993). *Adolescence: An Introduction* (5th ed.). Dubuque, IA: Brown & Benchmark Publishers.

GENERAL INFORMATION ABOUT OVERWEIGHT

Kolata, G. (1989). The business of thinness. *Encyclopaedia Britannica. Medical and Health Annual 1989.* Chicago: Encyclopaedia Britannica, Inc.

Landau, E. (1991). *Weight: A Teenage Concern.* New York: Lodestar Books.

Silverstein, A., Silverstein, V. B., & Silverstein, R. (1991). *So You Think You're Fat?* New York: Harper Collins Publishers.

Williams, J. A. (1990). Calorie counting—The scientific way. *Encyclopaedia Britannica. Medical and Health Annual 1990.* Chicago: Encyclopaedia Britannica, Inc.

DIETING AND OVERWEIGHT CONTROL: PROBLEMS

Bennett, W., & Gurin, J. (1982). The Dieters Dilemma: Eating Less and Weighing More. New York: Basic Books.

Fitzgerald, F. I. (1985). Space-age snake oil: Obesity and consumer fraud. *Postgraduate Medicine 78,* 231–240.

Foreyt, J. P., & Goodrick, G. K. (1992). *Living Without Dieting*. Houston, TX: Harrison Publishing.

Garner, D. M., & Wooley, S. C. (1991). Confronting the failure of behavioral and dietary treatments for obesity. *Clinical Psychology Review 11*, 729–780.

Polivy, J., & Herman, C. P. (1983). *Breaking the Diet Habit*. New York: Basic Books.

EATING DISORDERS

Bruch, H. (1979). *The Golden Cage: The Enigma of Anorexia Nervosa*. New York: Vintage Books.

Schlundt, D. G., & Johnson, W. G. (1990). *Eating Disorders: Assessment and Treatment*. Boston: Allyn & Bacon.

EATING SENSIBLY

Christian, J. L., & Gregor, J. L. (1991). *Nutrition for Living* (3rd ed.). Menlo Park, CA: Benjamin–Cummings Publishing Company.

Deutsch, R. M. (1977). *The New Nuts among the Berries*. Palo Alto: Bull Publishing.

Deutsch, R. M. (1978). *The Fat Counter Guide*. Palo Alto: Bull Publishing.

Editors. (1993, May). No-fat foods. *Consumer Reports 58*, 279–283.

Human Nutrition Information. (1992). *The Food Guide Pyramid*. Home and Garden Bulletin No. 252 (contact: USDA's Human Nutrition Information Service at U.S. Department of Agriculture, Human Nutrition Information Service, 6505 Belcrest Road, Hyattsville, MD 20782).

EXERCISING

Freedson, P. S., Rippe, J., & Ward, A. (1989). Turning kids on to fitness. *Encyclopaedia Britannica. Medical and Health Annual 1990.* Chicago: Encyclopaedia Britannica, Inc.

Sharkey, B. J. (1984). *Physiology of Fitness* (2nd ed.). Champaign: Human Kinetics.

OVERWEIGHT CONTROL

Epstein, L. H., & Squires, S. (1988). *The Stoplight Diet for Children.* Boston: Little, Brown & Company.

Kirschenbaum, D. S., Johnson, W. G., & Stalonas, P. M. (1987). *Treating Childhood and Adolescent Obesity.* New York: Pergamon Press.

LeBow, M. D. (1991). *Overweight Children.* New York: Insight Books.

REFERENCES ━━━━━━━━━━━━━━━

CHAPTER 1

1. Dietz, W. H. (1990). You are what you eat—What you eat is what you are. *Journal Adolescent Health Care 11*, 76–81.
2. LeBow, M. D. (1981). *Weight Control: The Behavioral Strategies*. New York: John Wiley & Sons.
3. LeBow, M. D. (1981).
4. LeBow, M. D. (1981).
5. LeBow, M. D. (1981).

CHAPTER 2

1. Dietz, W. H. (1990). You are what you eat—what you eat is what you are. *Journal Adolescent Health Care 11*, 76–81.
2. Stunkard, A. J., Sorensen, T., Hanis, C., Teasdale, T. W., Chakraborty, R., Schull, W. J., & Schulsinger, F. (1986). An adoption study of human obesity. *New England Journal of Medicine 314*, 193–198.
3. Stunkard, A. J. (1991). Genetic contributions to human obesity. *Research Publication of the Association for Nervous and Mental Diseases 69*, 205–218.
4. Powers, P. S. (1980). *Obesity: The Regulation of Weight*. Baltimore: Williams & Wilkins.
5. Wilkinson, J. F. (1980). *Don't Raise Your Child to Be a Fat Adult*. Indianapolis: Bobbs-Merrill.

6. Deutsch, R. (1976). *Realities of Nutrition.* Palo Alto: Bull Publishing.

7. National Research Council. (1989). *Recommended Dietary Allowances* (10th ed.). Washington, DC: National Academy Press.

8. Foreyt, J. P., & Goodrick, G. K. (1992). *Living Without Dieting.* Houston, TX: Harrison Publishing.

CHAPTER 3

1. Davis, J. (1980). *Garfield at Large: His First Book.* New York: Ballantine Books.

2. Brownell, K. D. (1991). Dieting and the search for the perfect body: where physiology and culture collide. *Behavior Therapy 22,* 1–12.

3. Kirkley, B. G., & Burge, J. C. (1989). Dietary restriction in young women: Issues and concerns. *Annals of Behavioral Medicine 11,* 66–72.

4. Garner, D. M., Garfinkel, P. E., Schwartz, D., & Thompson, M. (1980). Cultural expectations of thinness in women. *Psychological Reports 47,* 483–496.

5. Blackburn, G. L., & Pavlou, K. (1983). Fad reducing diets: Separating fads from facts. *Contemporary Nutrition 8,* 349–351.

6. Rees, J. M. (1990). Management of obesity in adolescence. *Adolescent Medicine, Medical Clinics of North America 74,* 1275–1292.

7. Foreyt, J. P., & Goodrick, G. K. (1992). *Living Without Dieting.* Houston, TX: Harrison Publishing.

8. Fitzgerald, F. I. (1985). Space-age snake oil: Obesity and consumer fraud. *Postgraduate Medicine 78,* 231–240.

9. Blackburn, G. L., & Pavlou, K. (1983).

10. Kolata, G. (1989). The business of thinness. *Encyclopaedia Britannica. Medical and Health Annual 1989.* Chicago: Encyclopaedia Britannica, Inc.

11. Mayer, J. (1977). *A Diet for Living*. New York: Pocket Books.
12. Kirkley, B. G., & Burge, J. C. (1989).
13. Brownell, K. D., Greenwood, M. R. C., Stellar, E., & Shrager, E. E. (1986). The effects of repeated cycles of weight loss and regain in rats. *Physiology and Behavior 38*, 459–464.
14. Wadden, T. A., Bartlett, S., Letizia, K. A., Foster, G. D., & Stunkard, A. J. (1992). Relationship of dieting history to resting metabolic rate, body composition, eating behavior, and subsequent weight loss. *American Journal of Clinical Nutrition 56*, 203s–208s.
15. Brownell, K. D., & Rodin, J. (1994). Medical, metabolic, and psychological effects of weight dieting. *Archives of Internal Medicine 154*, 1323–1330.
16. Rodin, J., Radke-Sharpe, N., Rebuffe-Scrive, M., & Greenwood, M. R. C. (1990). Weight cycling and fat distribution. *International Journal of Obesity 14*, 303–310.
17. Lapidus, L., & Bengtsson, C. (1988). Regional obesity as a health hazard in women—A prospective study. *Acta Medica Scandinavica, Supplementum 723*, 53–71.
18. American Psychiatric Association. (1994). *Diagnostic and Statistical Manual of Mental Disorders: Fourth Edition*. Washington, DC: American Psychiatric Association.
19. Schlundt, D. G., & Johnson, W. G. (1990). *Eating Disorders: Assessment and Treatment*. Boston: Allyn & Bacon.
20. Schlundt, D. G., & Johnson, W. G. (1990).
21. Mayer, J. (1977).
22. Christian, J. L., & Gregor, J. L. (1991). *Nutrition for Living* (3rd ed.). Menlo Park, CA: Benjamin–Cummings Publishing Company.
23. National Research Council. (1989). *Recommended Dietary Allowances* (10th ed.). Washington, DC: National Academy Press.

24. Human Nutrition Information. (1992). *The Food Guide Pyramid*. Home and Garden Bulletin No. 252. Human Nutrition Information Service, USDA.
25. National Research Council. (1989).

CHAPTER 4

1. DuRant, R. H., & Linder, C. W. (1981). An evaluation of five indices of relative body weight for use with children. *Journal of the American Dietetic Association 78*, 35–41.
2. Dwyer, J., & Mayer, J. (1975). The dismal condition: Problems faced by obese adolescent girls in American society. In G. Bray (Ed.), *Obesity in Perspective* (DHEW Publication No. [NIH] 75-708, pp. 103–110). Washington, DC: Superintendent of Documents, U.S. Government Printing Office Stock No. 017-053-00046-9.
3. Kirschenbaum, D. S., Johnson, W. G., & Stalonas, P. M. (1987). *Treating Childhood and Adolescent Obesity*. New York: Pergamon Press.
4. Foreyt, J. P., & Goodrick, G. K. (1981). Childhood obesity. In E. Mash & L. Terdal (Eds.), *Behavioral Assessment of Childhood Disorders*. New York: The Guilford Press.
5. Buckmaster, L., & Brownell, K. D. (1988). The social and psychological world of the obese child. In N. A. Krasnegor, G. D. Grave, & N. Kretchmer (Eds.), *Childhood Obesity: A Biobehavioral Perspective*. Caldwell, NJ: The Telford Press.
6. Cohen, F., Gelfand, D., Dodd, D. Jensen, J., & Turner, C. (1980). Self-control practices associated with weight loss maintenance in children and adolescents. *Behavior Therapy 11*, 26–37.
7. Freedson, P. S., Rippe, J., & Ward, A. (1989). Turning kids on to fitness. *Encyclopaedia Britannica. Medical and Health Annual 1990*. Chicago: Encyclopaedia Britannica, Inc.

8. Christian, J. L., & Gregor, J. L. (1991). *Nutrition for Living* (3rd ed.). Menlo Park, CA: Benjamin-Cummings Publishing Company.

CHAPTER 5

1. American Diabetes Association, Inc., and the American Dietetic Association. (1986). *Exchange Lists for Meal Planning*. Alexandria, VA: The American Diabetes Association. Chicago: The American Dietetic Association.
2. Stuart, R. B., & Davis, B. A. (1978). *Slim Chance in a Fat World. Condensed Edition Revised.* Champaign: Research Press.
3. Epstein, L. H. (1988). The Pittsburgh childhood weight control program. In N. A. Krasnegor, G. D. Grave, & N. Kretchmer (Eds.), *Childhood Obesity: A Biobehavioral Perspective.* Caldwell, NJ: The Telford Press.
4. Epstein, L. H., & Squires, S. (1988). *The Stoplight Diet for Children.* Boston: Little, Brown, & Company.
5. Kirschenbaum, D. S., Johnson, W. G., & Stalonas, P. M. (1987). *Treating Childhood and Adolescent Obesity.* New York: Pergamon Press.
6. Dietz, W. H. (1990). You are what you eat—What you eat is what you are. *Journal Adolescent Health Care 11,* 76–81.
7. Tucker, L. A. (1986). The relationship of television viewing to physical fitness and obesity. *Adolescence 21,* 797–806.
8. Dietz, W. H. (1990); Dietz, W. H. (1986). Prevention of childhood obesity. *Pediatric Clinics of North America 33,* 823–833.
9. Dietz, W. H. (1990).
10. Collipp, P. J. (1980). Long Island child life program. In P. J. Collipp (Ed.), *Childhood Obesity* (2nd ed.). Littleton, MA: PSG Publishing.

CHAPTER 6

1. Foxx, R. M. (1972). Social reinforcement of weight reduction: A case report on an obese retarded adolescent. *Mental Retardation 10*, 21–23.
2. Writing Tools Group. (1991). *The American Heritage Dictionary*. Sausalito, CA: Writing Tools Group, Inc.
3. Cautela, J. R., Cautela, J., & Esonis, S. (1983). *Forms for Behavior Analysis with Children*. Champaign: Research Press.
4. Bruch, H. (1973). *Eating Disorders*. New York: Basic Books.
5. DiScipio, W. J., Paul, H., & Byers, A. C. (1976). *Applied social behavior analysis of overeating in hospitalized psychotic girls*. Paper presented at the meeting of the Association of Behavior Analysis, Chicago.
6. Stuart, R. B. (1967). Behavioral control of overeating. *Behaviour Research and Therapy 5*, 357–365.

CHAPTER 7

1. Mahoney, M. J., & Mahoney, K. (1976). *Permanent Weight Control*. New York: W. W. Norton & Co.
2. Kirschenbaum, D. S., Johnson, W. G., & Stalonas, P. M. (1987). *Treating Childhood and Adolescent Obesity*. New York: Pergamon Press.
3. Beck, A. T., Rush, A. J., Shaw, B. F., & Emery, G. (1979). *Cognitive Therapy of Depression*. New York: The Guilford Press.
4. Coates, T. J., Jeffery, R. N., Slinkard, L. A., Killen, J. D., & Danaher, B. G. (1982). Frequency of contact and monetary reward in weight loss, lipid change, and blood pressure reduction with adolescents. *Behavior Therapy 13*, 175–185.
5. Alberti R. E., & Emmons M. L. (1970). *Your Perfect Right*. San Luis Obispo: Impact Publishers.

CHAPTER 8

1. Foreyt, J. P., & Goodrick, G. K. (1992). *Living Without Dieting.* Houston, TX: Harrison Publishing.
2. Bruch, H. (1973). *Eating Disorders.* New York: Basic Books.
3. Mayer, J., Roy, P., & Mitra, K. P. (1956). Relation between calorie intake, body weight, and physical work: Studies in an industrial male population in West Bengal. *American Journal of Clinical Nutrition 4*, 169–175.

CHAPTER 9

1. Landau, E. (1991). *Weight: A Teenage Concern.* New York: Lodestar Books.
2. Wadden, T. A., Stunkard, A. J., Rich, L., Rubin, C. J., Sweidel, G., & McKinney, S. (1990). Obesity in black adolescent girls: A controlled clinical trial of treatment by diet, behavior modification, and parental support. *Pediatrics 85*, 345–351.
3. Keesey, R. K., & Corbett, S. W. (1984). Metabolic defense of the body weight set-point. In A. J. Stunkard & E. Stellar (Eds.), *Eating and Its Disorders.* New York: Raven Press.
4. Keys, S., Brozek, J., Heneschel, A., Mickelson, O., & Taylor, H. L. (1950). *The Biology of Human Starvation* (Vols. 1 & 2). Minneapolis: University of Minnesota Press.
5. Sims, E. A. H., & Horton, E. S. (1968). Endocrine and metabolic adaptation to obesity and starvation. *American Journal of Clinical Nutrition 21*, 1455–1470.
6. Silverstein, A., Silverstein, V. B., & Silverstein, R. (1991). *So You Think You're Fat?* New York: Harper Collins Publishers.

CHAPTER 10

1. Stunkard, A. J. (1976). *The Pain of Obesity*. Palo Alto: Bull Publishing.
2. Brownell, K. D., Kelman, J., & Stunkard, A. J. (1983). Treatment of obese children with and without their mothers: Changes in weight and blood pressure. *Pediatrics 71*, 515–523.
3. Wadden, T. A., Stunkard, A. J., Rich, L., Rubin, C. J., Sweidel, G., & McKinney, S. (1990). Obesity in black adolescent girls: A controlled clinical trial of treatment by diet, behavior modification, and parental support. *Pediatrics 85*, 345–351.
4. Brownell, K. D. (1987). *The Learn Program for Weight Control*. Philadelphia: K. D. Brownell, Department ofPsychiatry.
5. Berg, F. M. (1983). *How to Be Slimmer, Trimmer & Happier*. Hettinger, ND: Flying Diamond Books.
6. Kirschenbaum, D. S., Johnson, W. G., & Stalonas, P. M. (1987). *Treating Childhood and Adolescent Obesity*. New York: Pergamon Press.
7. Ikeda, J. (1978). *For Teenagers Only: Change Your Habits to Change Your Shape*. Palo Alto: Bull Publishing; Ikeda, J. (1987). *Winning Weight Loss for Teens*. Palo Alto: Bull Publishing.
8. Mellin, L. M. (1991). *Shapedown: Weight Management Program of Children and Adolescents* (5th ed.). San Anselmo, CA: Balboa Publishing; Mellin, L. M., Slinkard, L. A., & Irwin, C. E. (1987). Validation of the shapedown program. *Journal of the American Dietetic Association 87*, 333–338.
9. Gortmaker, S. L., Dietz, W. H., Sobol, A. M., & Wehler, C. A. (1987). Increasing pediatric obesity in the United States. *American Journal of Diseases in Children 141*, 535–540.
10. Himes, J. H. (1994). Guidelines for overweight in adolescent preventive services: Recommendations from an ex-

pert committee. *The American Journal of Clinical Nutrition 59*, 307–316.

11. Health and Welfare Canada. (1988). *Promoting Healthy Weights* (#H39-131/1988e). Ottawa: Minister of National Health and Welfare.

12. Van Itallie, T. B. (1985). Health implications of overweight and obesity in the United States. *Annals of Internal Medicine 103*, 983–988.

13. Messerli, F. H. (1984). Obesity in hypertension: How innocent a bystander? *The American Journal of Medicine 77*, 1077–1082.

14. Van Itallie, T. B. (1985).

15. Berg, F. M. (1993). *Health Risks of Obesity: Special Report* (p. 117). Hettinger, ND: Obesity & Health.

16. Simopoulos, A. (1986). Obesity and body weight standards. *Annual Review of Public Health 7*, 481–492.

17. National Institutes of Health Consensus Development Conference Statement. (1985). *Health Implications of Obesity 5*. U.S. Government Printing Office.

18. National Institutes of Health Consensus Development Conference Statement. (1985).

19. Garner, D. M., & Wooley, S. C. (1991). Confronting the failure of behavioral and dietary treatments for obesity. *Clinical Psychology Review 11*, 729–780.

20. Berg, F. M. (1993). *The Health Risks of Weight Loss.* Hettinger, ND: Obesity & Health.

21. Castiglia, P. T. (1989). Obesity in adolescence. *Journal of Pediatric Health Care 3*, 221–223.

22. Wadden, T. A., Stunkard, A. J., Rich, L., Rubin, C. J., Sweidel, G., & McKinney, S. (1990).

23. Rocchini, A. P. (1992). Adolescent obesity and cardiovascular risk. *Pediatric Annals 21*, 235–240.

24. Wabitsch, W., Hauner, H., Blockmann, A., Parthon, W., Maye, H., & Teller, W. (1992). The relationship between

body fat distribution and weight loss in obese adolescent girls. *International Journal of Obesity 16*, 905–912.

25. Rocchini, A. P. (1992).

26. Must, A., Jacque, P. F., Dallal, G. E., Bajema, C. J., & Dietz, W. H. (1992). Long-term morbidity of overweight adolescents: A follow-up of the Harvard Growth Study of 1922 to 1935. *The New England Journal of Medicine 327*, 1350–1355.

27. Bray, G. A. (1992). Adolescent overweight may be tempting fate. *The New England Journal of Medicine 327*, 1379–1380.

28. Must, A., Jacque, P. F., Dallal, G. E., Bajema, C. J., & Dietz, W. H. (1992).

29. Brody, J. E. (1992). Adolescent obesity linked to adult ailments. *The New York Times National* (Thursday, November 5).

INDEX